D1202530

# LIVING
# A COURSE
# *in*
# MIRACLES

# LIVING
# A COURSE
*in*
# MIRACLES

*An Essential Guide
to the Classic Text*

## JON MUNDY, PhD

STERLING ETHOS
New York

STERLING ETHOS
New York

An Imprint of Sterling Publishing
387 Park Avenue South
New York, NY 10016

© 2011 by Jon Mundy

ISBN 978-1-4549-0000-9

Distributed in Canada by Sterling Publishing
$c/o$ Canadian Manda Group, 165 Dufferin Street
Toronto, Ontario, Canada M6K 3H6
Distributed in the United Kingdom by GMC Distribution Services
Castle Place, 166 High Street, Lewes, East Sussex, England BN7 1XU
Distributed in Australia by Capricorn Link (Australia) Pty. Ltd.
P.O. Box 704, Windsor, NSW 2756, Australia

For information about custom editions, special sales, and premium and corporate
purchases, please contact Sterling Special Sales at 800-805-5489 or
specialsales@sterlingpublishing.com.

The ideas expressed herein are those of the author and do not reflect an endorsement
of the Foundation for Inner Peace, the publishers of *A Course in Miracles*.

Manufactured in the United States of America

8  10  9

www.sterlingpublishing.com

*This course can be summed up very simply in this way:*
**Nothing real can be threatened.**
**Nothing unreal exists.**
*Herein lies the peace of God.*

From the Introduction to *A Course in Miracles*

✳

# Table of Contents

Referencing *A Course in Miracles* and A Definition of Terms    xi

## PART I
### BASIC TERMS AND CONCEPTS

CHAPTER 1    **There Must Be Another Way**     **3**
How It Came to Be

CHAPTER 2    **Inward Is Sanity**     **12**
Selfishness, Aloneness, and Insanity

CHAPTER 3    **This Is It!**     **18**
An Introduction to *A Course in Miracles*

CHAPTER 4    **The Story of Salvation**     **25**
The Main Characters

CHAPTER 5    **From Mindlessness to Mindfulness**     **33**
How the Mind Works According to
*A Course in Miracles*

CHAPTER 6    **The Dynamics of the Ego**     **47**
Demythologizing Adam and Eve

CHAPTER 7    **The Undoing of Guilt**     **59**
Our Way Out of Fear

# PART II
## THE METAPHYSICS OF MIRACLES

CHAPTER 8    **The Dreaming of the World**                    76
             The Metaphysics of Miracles

CHAPTER 9    **I Am Not a Body**                              86
             Death and the Ego Body Identity

CHAPTER 10   **Always Must Be Now**                           98
             The Practice of Patience

# PART III
## LIVING *A COURSE IN MIRACLES*
## THE PRACTICAL APPLICATION

CHAPTER 11   **The Inner Teacher, the Ego,**
             **and God's Plan for Salvation**                 114
             The Role of the Holy Spirit in *A Course in Miracles*

CHAPTER 12   **Why Is This Happening to Me?**                 125
             Trial, Accidents, Coincidence, and Destiny

CHAPTER 13   **Self-Observation**                             133
             Watching, Witnessing, and Willingness

CHAPTER 14   **Everyone Has the Answer Now**                  145
             Remembering What We Already Know

CHAPTER 15    **Healing the T(error)ist Within**          155
              On Anger and Responsibility

CHAPTER 16    **From Selfishness to Self-fullness**       171
              I'm Nobody. Who Are You?

CHAPTER 17    **Above All Else**                          191
              Strengthening Motivation to Change

CHAPTER 18    **A Course in Mind Training**               201
              Changing Our Minds—Changing Our Lives

CHAPTER 19    **Word Fasting: The Spiritual Diet**        216
              Observing and Correcting Our Thoughts

CHAPTER 20    **There Is Nothing to Forgive**             233
              Or, There Is No Future in the Past

CHAPTER 21    **The Key Marked Kindness**                 246
              As We Teach, So Do We Learn


Postscript: Living *A Course in Miracles*                 253
Resources                                                 255
Acknowledgments                                           259
About the Author                                          260

# Referencing *A Course in Miracles*

Quotations and paraphrasing from *A Course in Miracles* are from the third edition published by the Foundation for Inner Peace. The location of the various quotes and paraphrases appear immediately after the reference with a listing of the chapter, section, paragraph and sentence as in (T-4.III.5:7). A centered, italicized quote with no reference is from me.

**T:** is for *Text*
**W:** is for *Workbook*
**M:** is for *Manual for Teachers*
**C:** is for *Clarification of Terms*
**P:** is for *Psychology: Purpose, Process and Practice*
**S:** is for *The Song of Prayer*
**In:** is for *Introduction*
**R:** is for *Review*

Quotations from the Bible are from the King James Version, the same version referenced within the Course.

# A Definition of Terms

When you see a paragraph with the first few words in bold that includes the word "is," this is a definition of a term frequently used in the Course.

# PART I

# Basic Terms
# and Concepts

*

# CHAPTER 1

# There Must Be Another Way

## HOW IT CAME TO BE

*A good teacher clarifies his own ideas,*
*and strengthens them by teaching them.*

T-4.I.1:1

*A Course in Miracles* is the wisest, sanest, deepest book I know. It is a unique spiritual document; a self-instructional textbook, eloquent in its loveliness and level of psychological sophistication. It is a modern spiritual classic regarded by many as the most important book since the Bible. It is clearly a document of the twentieth and the twenty-first centuries, simultaneously simple and erudite. It calls for a *wholly* different way of seeing, completely outside the realm of what we call the ego and physical sight. It is also an immanently practical book, as it is trying to help us to stop the mind's insane machinations, heal all distorted frames of reference, and regain control of our right mind. It helps in the development of trust, honesty, tolerance, gentleness, joy, defenselessness, generosity, patience, faithfulness, open-mindedness, and more. Pick up the Course, open it to any page and read. Chances are the word "you" will appear on that page. The Course was written for you! Reading the Course, you feel as though you have returned home and you are now conversing with a long lost friend, you are being reintroduced to something very familiar—your True Self.

## A Radical Philosophy

The Course is a radical philosophy in that it asks us to engage in a total reversal in thinking. Our perception, it says, is upside down and backwards. We are to stop looking for the inside on the outside. We are to do a complete 180. We are learning to see the world in a wholly new light, no longer from the perspective of the ego. Rather now do we see wholly from the realm of Spirit. Radical means "root" and the Course is taking us all the way to the core of our most basic problem— "the minds decision for the ego." At this point and this point only, can we undo mistaken perception "choose once again" and begin to follow a path that leads us home.

Living the Course means we stop blaming ourselves and thus inevitably we cease blaming others. Living the Course means gaining freedom from judgment, anger, and condemnation. It means freedom from guilt and fear. The goal of the Course is peace and happiness. It aims at taking us all the way to Heaven. Pick up the Course, turn to any page, start reading, and you'll soon say, "Wow! Who wrote this?" What we have is a clear reflection of the truth, beautifully written, and, if we have the ears to hear—it is also impeccably clear.

*Simplicity is very difficult for twisted minds.*

T-14.II.2:3

The Course makes no effort to teach what cannot be easily understood. It is simple, direct, and straightforward. It pulls no punches. Truth is true. Truth is simple. What's not simple is that we are not simple. Our minds are convoluted. Truth is consistent. We're inconsistent. We try to give part of our allegiance to God (Love), and part to the ego (fear); and we fall off into the middle.

*The lessons you have taught yourself have been*
*so overlearned and fixed they rise like heavy curtains*
*to obscure the simple and the obvious.*

T-31.I.3:3–4

Although the Course is simple, it is easy to read the Course and not understand or be willing to accept it. We don't hear or "get" the Course because we have so over-learned the lessons of the ego and we are so accustomed to its voice, we don't even know there is another voice—a voice of reason and sanity. We don't hear the Course because we don't want to. As with all recalcitrant children, we have an authority problem. Who among us wants to hear that the self we made and the world we have made to go with it is not real? Living the Course means I'm going to have to completely lay aside the idea of a separate, independent self, and who wants to do that?

*The world you seem to live in is not home to you.*
*And somewhere in your mind you know that this is true.*

W-182.1:1–2

Imagine, for a moment, that there is a dictator, a despot, a tormenter who seeks possession of your mind. We think we have freedom, that we can do whatever we want; and yet, this thing we call an ego can take over the mind so that we are not even aware that it has taken control. Still, no matter how great the seduction, there remains something in the back of the mind which says: "This isn't it. The world you see is not reality. There must be another way."

*Belief that there is another way of perceiving is the loftiest idea*
*of which ego thinking is capable. That is because it contains*
*a hint of recognition that the ego is not the Self.*

T-4.II.4:10–11

## The Story of the Course

The Course began in 1965, with Dr. Helen Schucman and Dr. William Thetford, professors of medical psychology at Columbia University's College of Physicians and Surgeons in New York. Frustrated by the competitiveness and infighting that characterized their relationship one day Bill turned to his assistant Helen and said, "There has to be another way," meaning, there has to be some way that they could get along without all the backstabbing, fighting, and ego games that trouble many offices, hospitals, schools, businesses, churches, and families throughout the world. Unexpectedly, Helen turned back to Bill and said, "You're right—and I'll help you find it." With this sudden willingness to drop defensiveness, a common ground for healing was born. Through Helen and Bill's unified decision to heal, the seeds for the Course found fertile soil and took root.

On October 21, 1965, while recording her thoughts in a notebook, Helen heard, "This is *A Course in Miracles*." Imagine you are a poet and you begin to hear a poem or imagine that you are composer and you begin to hear the notes of a song. It was not automatic writing. Nothing took control of Helen's hand and began writing for her. It was as though an inner voice was speaking to her. She could stop taking this *dictation* at any point, answer the phone, or take care of her other business and then return to the writing, as though there had been no interruption. Helen had the remarkable ability to simply "get out of her own way" and let Love—what we now call *A Course in Miracles*—flow through.

Helen took notes for seven years and completed the Course in September 1972. A 669 page *Text* explains the teachings of the Course. There is a *Workbook* for students, which consists of 365 daily lessons or exercises, and a ninety-two page *Manual for Teachers*. She also received two pamphlets from the same source as the Course: *The Song of Prayer,* and *Psychotherapy, Purpose, Process, and Practice.* All told, we're looking at just about a half-million words. The Course was published on June 22, 1976. More than two million copies have been sold. It is now available in eighteen different languages, and several additional translations are in process. Spanish is the next best-selling edition after English.

One of the unique qualities of the Course is the Workbook with its 365 daily lessons designed to help us break up our habituated ego-oriented ways of seeing the world. There is only one rule in the whole Course, and that is not to do more than one lesson per day, though you may want to spend more than a day on some of the lessons. What is called for is not speed, but practice.

In 1973, at a conference sponsored by Spiritual Frontier Fellowship, Helen and Bill attended a lecture I gave on mysticism, based on a book I had written, *Learning to Die.* That evening, I was introduced to the two of them. All I was told at that time was that Helen had written "an inspirational book." In 1974, while working on a dissertation on the relationship between psychology and spirituality, I wrote a letter that was published in the newsletter of the Association for Transpersonal Psychology, expressing interest in being in contact with anyone working in the field of psychotherapy and spirituality. Bill saw my letter, remembered our previous meeting, and suggested to Helen that it was a call for her to complete the writing of what is now simply called the Psychotherapy Pamphlet, which she had begun earlier but never completed.

Helen agreed, called me in April 1975, and said that she had something for me. I had no idea what she was talking about, but I agreed to meet with her and Bill, Father Benedict Groschel, and Dr. Kenneth Wapnick at Ken's little studio apartment on East 17th Street in New York City. I was, at the time, a doctoral student, university lecturer, and minister, living inside of the General Theological Seminary on West 19th Street, and I walked over that evening. Ken's little studio was one of the most basic apartments I had ever seen. There were no electronics, no whatnots; just a typewriter, a few books, a pot for tea, a towel, a toothbrush—the bare essentials.

Helen sat on Ken's daybed and told me about the Course, how it had come into existence, and how it had affected the four of them. Though I had explored several different philosophies, including a guru search and a backpacking trek through India in 1971, most everything left me wanting something more. Though impressed with my colleagues, I was concerned that I would again be left wanting. Still, I walked home that night thinking that *probably* the most important thing that had ever happened to me had just happened. I was, however, not at all sure what it was.

Later, Ken came to visit me at General Theological, and I began sponsoring lectures by Ken in New York City, Westchester, and Orange Counties in New York. He has been, throughout these many years, a wonderful older brother. Helen, in turn, became something of a "mother hen" and a guide in times of trouble. I would meet with Helen at either Judy Whitson's or Ken Wapnick's apartment and she was always available by phone. She knew, it seemed, how to quickly assess my situation and offer the right guidance. I was frequently in trouble in my relationships with women, and Helen was there to help me sort through my feelings. I was also ambiguous about my relationship with the Methodist church. While I felt called to be a minister, I kept thinking maybe I should quit. Helen kept saying, "Not yet. You can always quit later." Sixteen years later, I did.

## The Voice and Language of the Course

In reading the Course, it soon becomes clear that the Voice of the Course is not that of any ordinary individual. It is clearly not written by an ego. Pick it up—turn to any page and read. It is not about the past, the future, or worldly events. There is no "ax to grind." There is no agenda other than helping us achieve inner peace, and therefore our own greatest happiness. The Course is clear, truthful, and filled with compassion and understanding. Philosophy seeks the truth through argumentation. Though logically consistent throughout, there is no argumentation in the Course. There are no "proofs" for the existence of God. The Course simply reminds us of the Truth of Being. The Voice in the Course is Jesus, or the Holy Spirit, or Your Voice at your best. It is your Self, my Self, our Self—One Self, God, or Christ. It came from one healed Mind which is all of us in our own right mind.

*It is your voice to which you listen as He speaks to you.*

W-125.8:1

The Course uses the phrase "Son of God" to refer to every child of God. While there are two possible genders, in this world there is literally no division. What is whole is not divided. What we are talking about is mankind as a whole or better, spirit as a whole. If, when you read a sentence like: *"I am as God created me. His Son can suffer nothing. And I am His Son,"* if it feels more comfortable saying daughter or child; change it to daughter or to child. The purpose of the Course is to help us get in touch with the Christ (Self) within.

*. . . words are but symbols of symbols.*
*They are thus twice removed from reality.*

M-21.1:9

## Only Truth Is True—A Perennial Philosophy

The Course is one form of a universal curriculum (M-1.4:1) and a unique path on par with the wisdom of the world's most profound spiritual teachings. What the Course says is not new. How could the eternal be new? Mystics, masters, saints, and sages from all over the world and throughout the ages have talked about that which goes beyond perception. We find "themes," "songs," and "representations" of the Course in the world's oldest philosophies—the Advaita Vedanta philosophy of Hinduism, Buddhism, Gnosticism, Christian Mysticism, Sufism, German Idealism, American Transcendentalism, The New Thought Movement, Unity, Religious Science, Christian Science, and many more thousands of forms.

> *Whether the flower of mysticism blooms in India or in China,*
> *in Persia or on the Rhine, its fruit is one.*

GERMAN THEOLOGIAN, RUDOLF OTTO (1869–1937)

The Course is not a religion. There is no hierarchical organization based on the Course. There is no evangelism in the Course. It is not about getting the word out to the world. It is about getting the word in to the heart. Retaining the mind in the heart is *inwardness*. Letting the mind go out is *externalization*. If I evangelize, I must think that I am right and you need correction. If the words get in, it can then be lived in such a way that other folks will see the efficacy of the teaching and the world will be very subtly and effectively changed. Change comes not through revolt, it comes through revelation. The Course is, as its name implies, a spiritual study. If you have an organized religion, you have someone on top, someone on the bottom, others in the middle, and ego-games and jockeying for position. The Course is simply a self-help book, par excellence. It can be studied completely on its own. As it means healing all our relationships, it also means living the Course in relationship with everyone we meet.

**WARNING:**

A friend once told me that when he started going to Alcoholics Anonymous, someone told him that the program would mess up his drinking big time. In other words, if he stuck with the program, he would stop drinking. Stick with the Course and it will mess up the ego big time. We are going for nothing less than enlightenment.

## CHAPTER 2

# Inward Is Sanity

## Selfishness, Aloneness, and Insanity

There is a Danish story about a spider that lived high in the rafter of an old barn. One day, the spider decided to lower himself to a beam where he found the flies more prolific and more easily caught. He therefore decided to live permanently on this lower level. He spun for himself a comfortable web. One day he noticed the line down which he had come and said to himself that he no longer needed it. So he snapped it and destroyed the support for his whole web.

A tiny thread connects us with the infinite. We have come from God and we are returning Home to Him. Everyone wakes up someday. Everything eventually returns to its source. Coming into the world, we easily become fascinated with the world and we forget about the source. We look at that thread which connects us with the infinite and think, "That thing is in the way." We snap the line, and we go mad.

*As you look with open eyes upon your world*
*it must occur to you that you have withdrawn into insanity...*
*You communicate with no one, and you are as isolated from reality*
*as if you were alone in all the universe... God calls you and you*

*do not hear, for you are preoccupied with your own voice.*
*And the vision of Christ is not in your sight,*
*for you look upon yourself alone.*

T-13.V.6:1, 4 & 6–7

## 1. Our First Interest Is Ourselves

Let's be honest, we place ourselves at the center of the universe. Our self is our first concern. According to a study done on response reactions during times of disasters, reported in *Science News*, March 1, 2010, it was found that, not surprisingly, "our first reflexes are selfish." It's the way it is in the ego's world and it's been this way as long as there has been an "us," a "me," and an ego. Caring about ourselves, first and foremost, has given rise to the entire ego thought system. It's not that we're never altruistic, or think loving thoughts, or do loving things. Still, our first thought is for our comfort, our aches and pains, how our bodies looks, our need for satisfaction, our status in the community, our finances, our relationships, and more.

## 2. We Think We Are Alone in the Universe

*The ego is the mind's belief that it is completely on its own.*

T-4.II.8:4

There are billions of people on this planet, but that does not keep us from feeling isolated. When I fell in love with my high school sweetheart, I fell hard. Although I had a loving family and loved nature and the farm I grew up on, this love was wholly new and different. It was the most wonderful, overwhelming, and magnificent thing I had ever known. We want to melt, to merge, to fall back into Oneness—and I "fell" big time. We were young, and I wanted to wait until the completion of college before we got married. Needing, however, to get away from her alcoholic father and demanding mother while I was away at college, my girlfriend deliberately got pregnant and then ran away with another man. I was crushed—totally and completely. There was no getting her back. I felt abandoned by the only love I had ever known, and it was, I thought at the time, the only love I would ever know. Driving around in my car, I kept banging my fist on the steering wheel, crying, screaming, talking out loud to God, and thinking, "I am all alone. It's just me and the universe."

### 3. We're All Crazy

*This is an insane world, and do not underestimate the extent of its insanity. There is no area of your perception that it has not touched, and your dream is sacred to you. That is why God placed the Holy Spirit in you, where you placed the dream.*

T-14.I.2:6–8

The first time I saw those two airplanes fly into the World Trade Center Towers, the first thought that went through my mind was the beginning sentence above, "This is an insane world, and do not underestimate the extent of its insanity." There are many wonderful experiences in this world. At the top of the list is the love we feel that radiates from us to each other. Our eyes fall upon many lovely things: flowers, birds, mountains, oceans, and magnificent works of art. Our ears, with delight, are tuned to music, children laughing, kittens meowing, dogs barking, and the sweet voices of those we love. Our lips and tongues taste delicious food. Our hands reach out to each other, our pets, warm blankets, and more. And yet, all these things are what the body's eyes see, and we are yet to *remember* our true identity.

*For the memory of God can dawn only in a mind*
*that chooses to remember, and that has relinquished*
*the insane desire to control reality.*

T-12.VIII.5:3

When it comes to the ego's world, the Course calls for incredible realism; there is, it *seems*, a tyrant who wants to live within my mind. This tyrant tells me many crazy things; hiding and subterfuge are cool; greed is good; anger justified; and war inevitable. To say the world is insane is not to condemn it. It is simply to see things as they are within the ego's framework. Much of history is one battle after another, one tribe killing another tribe, one emperor squeezing out another emperor, one class suppressing another, one nation taking over another nation. As nineteenth-century transcendentalist Ralph Waldo Emerson (1803–1882), expressed it, "History is one damn thing after the other." Or, as English historian Edward Gibbon (1737–1794), author of *The Decline and Fall of the Roman Empire* said, "History is little more than the register of the crimes, follies, and misfortunes of mankind." The story of brother against brother is the oldest story in the Bible. As soon as we've got a body, we've got an ego; we've got projection and competition; and, we've got *trouble right here in River City*. (From *The Music Man* in case you did not remember.)

*The world has not yet experienced any comprehensive*
*reawakening or rebirth. Such a rebirth is impossible*
*as long as you continue to project or miscreate.*

T-2.I.3:7–8

The madness of the ego is seen in our great "tragedies." *I Claudius*, by Robert Graves (1895–1985), about the Roman emperors of the first century, tells a story of a convoluted web of lies and intrigue woven initially by Caesar Augustus's wife, Lydia. To be sure that her son, Tiberius, would become emperor, with complete self-absorption and unbridled ambition, she saw to the poisoning of all of her stepchildren, and even, it seems, Caesar himself. Caesar's last words were: "Did I play my part well in this tragedy?" He knew it was a tragedy. The story of the succeeding emperors is a thorny drama of scheming and murder. Nero even killed his mother because she tried to tell him what to do. There was such self-righteousness and such unhappiness. There was little in the way of innocence and simplicity. So it is for the tragedies of Shakespeare or any of the great dramatists, or a contemporary soap opera on daytime television. Throughout the story of history, we find misperception, insanity, and unhappiness. Rarely do we find enduring contentment and the presence of the peace of God. That would not make an interesting story.

## And Now for a Wholly New Vision

Despite the bleakness of this picture, what if you *knew* beyond any doubt that there is a you that transcends this illusory world? What if you *knew* that you were not an ego plagued with problems of guilt and shame; fear and loss? What if you *knew*, further, that the world we live in is a thought, a "consensus reality" made up by an enormous group of other egos, developed in fear over millions of years, not out of mean intent, but simply pieced together from our own collective desperation?

Knowing all of this, but at the same time feeling trapped in a body in space and time, what if you were now presented with a map—a G.P.S. system designed by God (God's Plan for Salvation, if you will) which could show you the way out of this maze—this matrix of unawareness—beyond the body and the ego to our real Home, our real Self, and a state of true Being? What if you *knew* that the Kingdom of God was within you? What if it was possible to know this, not at some future date, but right now? Coming to, and then helping us hold this awareness is the task, the purpose, and the promise of the Course. It is what every sincere student of the Course will tell you they come to know and/or know that they are coming to.

*Inward is sanity; insanity is outside.*

T-18.I.7:4

The center of a hurricane is perfectly quiet. On the outside, it is all chaos. When we are centered, we are peaceful. When we are angry and projecting, we are in a chaotic state. The Course is clear that peace is not found in any form of external searching. Health is inner peace. The contemplative traditions of all of our world's religions tell us of a place not of this world—a home not made with hands. Heaven is found in awakening, not in sleeping. When we awaken in the morning we see that we never went anywhere. We were simply lying in our bed dreaming. Awakening means that we "were" dreaming. Awakening is the realization that we never left Heaven. Heaven is not "coming" someday.

*Heaven is here. There is nowhere else.*
*Heaven is now. There is no other time.*

M-24.6:4–7

The main ingredient in happiness is freedom. Freedom is always "from" something. Freedom from wants and needs; freedom from addictions; freedom from anxiety and fears, pains of the body; poverty, lack, and bills; relationships in which one feels trapped; political tyranny; and more. Living the Course means seeking and finding freedom from something which paradoxically does not exist; it means freedom from an illusion, freedom from something we call an ego, something which contains no reality.

*Be not content with future happiness.*
*It has no meaning, and is not your just reward.*
*For you have cause for freedom now.*

T-26.VIII.9:1

===

# CHAPTER 3

# This Is It!

## AN INTRODUCTION TO *A COURSE IN MIRACLES*

*This is a course in miracles.*
*It is a required course.*
*Only the time you take it is voluntary.*
*Free will does not mean that you can establish the curriculum.*
*It means only that you can elect what you want to take at a given time.*
*The course does not aim at teaching the meaning of love,*
*for that is beyond what can be taught.*
*It does aim, however, at removing the blocks to the awareness*
*of love's presence, which is your natural inheritance.*
*The opposite of love is fear,*
*but what is all-encompassing can have no opposite.*
*This course can therefore be summed up very simply in this way:*
*Nothing real can be threatened. Nothing unreal exists.*
*Herein lies the peace of God.*

FROM THE INTRODUCTION TO *A COURSE IN MIRACLES*

T-IN.1:1–8 & 2:1–4

## This Is It!

I sometimes begin public lectures by telling a story about a soldier walking around in an army camp barrack. He goes over and picks up a piece of paper (at which point I will pick up a piece of paper). The soldier looks at the piece of paper and says, "That's not it." And he throws it down. (I throw down the piece of paper.) He then goes over and picks up another piece of paper. (I then pick up another piece of paper.) He says, "That's not it," and he throws that piece of paper down as well. (I do the same.) His supervising officer is watching him and decides the guy is probably deranged, so he sends him off to the army psychologist for an examination.

The psychologist examines him and decides that, indeed, he is deranged, so he writes out a letter of dismissal from the army. He hands it to him. The man takes the letter, looks at it and says, "Oh, this is it!" At which point, I hold up a copy of *A Course in Miracles* and say, "This is it!" I then quote the first line of the Course, "This is *a course in miracles*, it is a required course. Only the time you take it is voluntary" (T-in.1:1–3).

> *There is a course for every teacher of God.*
> *The form of the course varies greatly. So do the particular teaching*
> *aids involved. But the content of the course never changes.*
> *Its central theme is always, "God's Son is guiltless,*
> *and in his innocence is his salvation."*
>
> M-1.3:1–5

## This Is a "Course" in Miracles

I do not know of any spiritual tradition that does not say that this world is a classroom. Once I see myself as a student in a classroom, I can then do what all responsible students do. Rather than ignoring my assignment, rather than sleeping or cutting classes, I begin to learn my lessons so that someday I can graduate, and thus attain yet greater freedom. Ultimately, we are all here to learn, just like Jesus, or any enlightened master—how to become a teacher of God—which means remembering our identity as a child of God.

*Miracles are everyone's right, but purification is necessary first.*

T-1.I.7

We are here to learn how to "remove the blocks to an awareness of love's presence" (T-in.1:7). Seeking greater health in the body, we often begin by engaging in a process of purification. In the same way, the Course calls for a purification of mind. Our task is not to seek for love (truth) but to seek and find all the barriers we have built against love (truth). Living the Course thus means bringing the darkness to the light. It is not necessary to seek for what is true but we do need to seek for what is false (T-16.IV.6:1–2). Coming into this world, we sign up for a variety of courses which teach us exactly what we need to learn. These courses are referred to in the Course as our "special relationships."

**A special relationship is** "a device for limiting our self to a body and for limiting others to their bodies" (T-16.VI.4:4). Our primary special relationship is the one we have with our own bodies. We love them; we hate them—we think the body is who we are. The body is a learning device for the mind. Its sole purpose is to facilitate learning. Lesson 97 from the Workbook is an affirmation, *I am spirit* and it adds, "no body can contain spirit, nor impose a limitation God created not." We also develop special relationships with other people, animals, and things of the world. We place expectations or anticipations onto them about the way the other person is supposed to behave in relationship to us, and if they don't behave that way then we get to be upset. Special relationships are thus the classroom in which we practice forgiveness, and thereby remember love.

## It Is a "Required" Course

Helen Schucman, the scribe for *A Course in Miracles*, was a teacher, and when she first heard "This is *A Course in Miracles*," she responded with, "Presumably this course is an elective." And the answer was, "No it isn't. It's a definite requirement." When we go to school, we find a number of required courses along with electives. Certain classes are basic. *Life is a required course.* Like it or not, we wake up every morning in a classroom called life. There is no avoiding it. As much as we might like to pull the covers up over our heads and go back into unconsciousness, we cannot avoid the inevitable—we must get up and deal with the world. We must deal with our bodies; we must clean, clothe, and feed them. We must deal with each other. We must earn money and make our way through the world. Somewhere along the way, we hope to find some peace of mind.

There are many classes within this curriculum. I may take a class where I must learn to overcome an addiction like alcohol, drugs, smoking, overeating, pills, and more. Here is a special relationship called money and a variety of electives within this field; I might try gambling, or shopping, or overspending. Here is a class with a variety of special relationships called romance, marriage, and parenthood. Here is a class called career and work, and, within it, I find a number of forgiveness opportunities with employers, supervisors, subordinates, and fellow employees.

One sunny summer day, my wife, Dolores, and I went to a church picnic. I wanted to spend a little time with each person there, so I moved about, beginning each conversation the usual way by asking someone how they were doing and then after the usual "fine," or "okay," they would begin to tell a story. Everyone, it seemed, was going through something, some lesson, some physical ailment, some drama, some tragedy; some "somebody done me wrong" song. Each one was trying to deal with his or her own insanity and that of the other people in their lives. In essence, each was telling me about their special relationships and what his or her classroom looked like.

The time in which we take this course is voluntary. Free will does not mean that we can decide in advance what the curriculum will be. Indeed, the path for each of us is highly individualized (M-29.II.6). Freewill does mean, however, that we can elect what we want to take at a given time.

## Everything and Nothing

The Course has sometimes been referred to as the Christian Vedanta. It represents an absolute monistic or non-dualistic system. The Course distinguishes between two worlds: One (Heaven) is wholly real; the other (the ego's world) is wholly illusory. We think of these two worlds as the world of God—Love—Happiness—Joy—Truth—Eternity—Heaven; and, the world of Ego—Fear—Guilt—Pain—Death—Falsehood—Space—Time—Illusion. Heaven is reality and the ego is a dream; that is, something which appears to be happening within time. The Course is thus an all-or-nothing philosophy. Either perfect Love exists or it does not. Either God exists or there is no God. Perfection is not a matter of degree. Either we are whole or we are broken. Either truth is true or there is no truth. Only perfect Oneness exists and what is all encompassing cannot have an opposite.

> *Life and death, light and darkness,*
> *knowledge and perception, are irreconcilable.*

> T-3.VII.6:6

Fellow student/teacher, Ken Mallory, uses an illustration from the binary system of 0's and 1's, 0 is ego, 1 is Spirit. Ego is nothing. God (Spirit) is everything. It is impossible that God could split Himself off from Himself. Oneness is oneness not two-ness. God is in charge; always has been and will be. It may look as though we have "temporary" control of our own lives, but *ultimately*, that is not true; and only what is *ultimately* true is true.

The Manual for Teachers of the Course begins by describing ten characteristics of a Teacher of God. Each characteristic builds on the one before it and the first characteristic is trust. We are asked to place total trust in God and nothing else, because there is nothing else. This is our greatest happiness. Only in this way do we find inner peace.

> *You have very little trust in me as yet, but it will increase*
> *as you turn more and more often to me instead of*
> *to your ego for guidance.*

T-4.VI.3:1

An emissary of the English, political leader Oliver Cromwell (1599–1659) was sent to France with his secretary to meet with King Louis XIV on some important business. Having crossed the English Channel, they spent the night at a seaport town. Concerned that things might not go well in the forthcoming meeting, the emissary tossed and turned all night, unable to sleep. He finally awakened his secretary, who was sleeping soundly. The emissary asked the secretary how it was possible that he could be sleeping so soundly while he, the emissary could not sleep. "Master," said the secretary, "May I ask a question?" "Yes," replied the emissary. "Did God rule the universe before we were born?" "Most assuredly He did," answered the emissary. "And will He rule it after we're dead?" continued the secretary. "Certainly, He will," said the emissary. "Then, master, why not let him rule the present?"

*The new beginning now becomes the focus of the curriculum.*
*The goal is clear, but now you need specific methods for attaining*
*it. The speed by which it can be reached depends on this one thing*
*alone: your willingness to practice every step.*
*Each one will help a little, every time it is attempted.*
*And together will these steps lead you from dreams of judgment to*
*forgiving dreams and out of pain and fear.*

T-30.IN.1:1—5

# CHAPTER 4

# The Story of Salvation

## THE MAIN CHARACTERS

*A myth is an image in terms of which*
*we try to make sense of the world.*

ALAN WATTS (1915–1973, U.S.)

The Gospel of Matthew says that Jesus *never* spoke without using parables. In fact, Matthew says, "He *always* taught using parables" (Matthew 13:34). According to the American mythologist Joseph Campbell (1904–1987), the one great story played out in all of mythic literature is the monomyth. Life is not just a matter of sleeping, eating, earning a living, raising a family, and dying. A hero or heroine is called to go forth on a search from the world of "everydayness" to the fulfillment of a spiritual destiny. The hero or heroine is looking to fulfill a mission often understood as finding the entrance to the Kingdom of Heaven. Inevitably, a variety of trials and difficulties are encountered along the way and the hero falls prey to the tricks of his own ego. Often, as in the story of the prodigal son, the hero experiences some sort of failure, some "crash and burn," some sort of emotional breakdown and breakthrough. Having reached the bottom of the pit and giving up on doing things on his own, the hero comes to awakening, surrenders his own will, and turns things over to a higher authority. In many stories, the hero or heroine encounters a guide, a book, a map, a teaching; or, they simply become more deeply aware of their own Inner Teacher.

This "guide" shows the hero or the heroine the way home through a process of gradual purification, a relinquishing of the old ways, and a reunification of the spiritual Self. The task is to integrate their new wisdom into practical everyday life. Though the pathway is highly individualized, it leads everyone ultimately to Oneness—Love—Truth—Home—God— Eternity, all such words being synonyms.

## A Very Old Story—The Hymn of the Pearl

B efore we look into the "story" of the Course, let's look at a brief rendition of one of the oldest stories in the world. Reflective of the message in *A Course in Miracles*, *The Hymn of the Pearl* is an old Syrian story, even much older than the third-century text, *The Acts of Thomas*, in which it is found.

> A young man dwells in a marvelous, rich kingdom. His parents send him on a mission with provisions, "great yet light," so that he can carry them. Before he leaves, he removes his Robe of Glory and splendid mantle. In his heart is inscribed a message concerning his mission. He is to obtain a pearl of wisdom lying in the middle of a sea encircled by a snorting serpent.

> Making his way downward, he is accompanied, at first, by two royal envoys. The way is dangerous and hard, and he is young. Having reached this new world, he disguises himself in a body like those around him and he keeps to himself until he recognizes an older "anointed one," with whom he develops a mutual trust. His friend tries to warn him about the "unclean" ones who, when they see that he is not a countryman, ingratiate themselves against him. But he falls

prey to the unclean ones, who, with cunning, mix drinks and give him their meat. He falls asleep and becomes unaware of his mission. He forgets that he is a king's son; he forgets the pearl of wisdom.

His parents learn of all that befalls their son and write a letter that calls him to awaken, rise out of sleep, break free of his bondage, and remember his destiny. The letter comes in the form of an eagle, which "becomes wholly speech." At its voice, he awakens, embraces the letter, breaks its seal, and recalls in his heart the words of his Father. He remembers that he is a king's son, a "freeborn soul." He remembers the pearl and the snorting serpent. Going to the serpent, he charms it to sleep by repeating to it his Father's name. Seizing the pearl, he repairs for home, leaving behind his "impure garments."

The voice of the letter now guides him with its light, discourages his fears, and with its light, draws him homeward. He had forgotten the "Robe of Glory" he had left behind in his youth. Seeing it again, it becomes a mirror image of himself. "Myself entirely I saw in it, and it entirely I saw in myself." Clothed in his robe, he ascends to the gates of salutation and adores the splendor of his Father, who had sent him on the mission and whose command he has now fulfilled.

Let's interpret (demythologize) this story. We come into this world—retaining in our heart the memory of our parents who send us on a mission. We are to discover (remember) our True Identity as a freeborn soul (Spirit). Disguising ourselves in bodies like those around us, the "unclean ones" (the ego-driven world), mix drinks with cunning and give us their meat—they tell us their story of the world and seduce us into dreaming their dream. Becoming enamored with the dream world, we fall into mindlessness and think our dream is reality. We forget our mission; we forget that we are in fact, Children of God. Our parents, seeing that we sleep, write a letter that calls us to awaken. The letter might be the

Bible, the Qur'an, the Vedas, the Tao Te Ching, *A Course in Miracles*, or any *form* of inspiration or wisdom teaching. The Voice of the letter "becomes wholly speech," and upon hearing its message, we begin our awakening. Charming the serpent (the ego) to sleep, we regain the pearl of wisdom, and in remembrance of our True Identity as "freeborn souls," we leave behind our impure garments (our bodies) and return Home to our Father.

## Introducing the "Characters" in the Play

Operas sometimes begin with an opening overture or scenes that are going to come. Let's begin by familiarizing ourselves with some words organized not alphabetically but rather by way of an outline of the basic story and practical teachings of the Course. Let's look at the *characters* in the play, the basic theme of the Course, the plot, and the solution to the problem presented in this "story."

**"God" is** one of the most frequent words in the Course. Helen described a dream/vision in which she found herself at the entrance to a cave. Going in, she found an old scroll. Opening the scroll she saw the words "God Is" in the center panel of the text. Little letters began to appear to the left and the right of the center panel, and she knew that by rolling the scroll to the left she would be able to look into the past, and by rolling the scroll to the right she would be able to look into the future. She decided, however, to leave it just where it was, and she heard a voice that said, "You made it that time. Thank you." We could just leave it as "God Is." The ego, the would-be culprit in our story, tempts us to roll out the scroll, and the moment we do, we are trapped in time—in a drama—in a story. Our drama is filled with an unending series of problems. Like a character in an Indiana Jones movie, we (the ego) go from one challenging adventure (problem) to another.

God (Love) is indescribable and far beyond our definition. The Buddha refused to define God, saying it could not be done. Try defining God. You can't do it. Define love. You can't do it.

The Course is trying to help us remember that which is formless and abstract. The ego would remind us of that which is concrete and delimited by space and time. The concrete part of the mind believes in the ego. The ego depends on the concrete (T-4.VII.1:4). God is divine abstraction. God is Mind. God is Life. God is Love. The more alive we are, the more in love we are; the more in love we are, the more alive we are—the more we know of God. Life—Love—Truth—God cannot be delimited. God, the giver of life, is described in the Course as the Father. The Father has a Son called Christ. "You" are the Son of God. We are all the sons and daughters of God. God's will for all of us is "perfect happiness," which is often described as peace, joy, innocence, and freedom.

**The Holy Spirit is** the Voice for God, the Christ Mind, the Light, the bridge to Heaven, and the communication link between us and God. It is a thought in my mind which helps me to understand my right-mind. It is thus a memory in the mind of God's Son. This memory has never been lost—only clouded over with our mindless dreaming of the world. The Holy Spirit is the "motivation" for miracle-mindedness. He is God's answer to the separation (T-5.II.2:5) and "the decision" to heal the separation. He sees our fearful perceptions and tries to help us through them. He is in us in a very literal sense (T-5.II.3–4). He is the Inner Teacher, comforter, guide, healer, and mediator.

> *The Voice of the Holy Spirit does not command,*
> *because It is incapable of arrogance. It does not demand,*
> *because It does not seek control. It does not overcome,*
> *because It does not attack. It merely reminds. It is compelling only*
> *because of what It reminds you of.*

T-5.II.7:1–5

**Jesus is** one who remembered who he was as Spirit. He remembered his identity—"I and the Father are one" (John 10:29–31). He was a man who saw the face of Christ, which is only goodness in all his brothers and sisters, and thus remembered God (C-5.2:1). Jesus is also the "I" in the Course, as in, "You can do anything I ask. I have asked you to perform miracles" (T-8:1–3).

**Christ is** the Son of God. As we are all the Sonship, we are also the Christ. Caught within the thought system of the ego, we do not, however, know (remember) our reality as Christ.

**You is** (normally, that would not be good English, but in this case, "you" is a character in the Course) the most frequently mentioned character in the Course, appearing 18,068 times. There are three you's in the Course.

1. Sometimes the Course refers to *you* as the ego. As in, "You think you are the home of evil, darkness, and sin" (W-93.1:1). This is the you of the body/personality.
2. Then there is the you that is the chooser or the observer. This is the *you* the Course is speaking to most of the time. This is the part which watches and decides between the ego and the Holy Spirit; between the wrong-mindedness and the right-mindedness.
3. Then there is the *You* that is the Self, the Son of God, the Christ, the You that is Oneness.

**The ego is** a *belief* or false concept we hold about ourselves. It is *a dream* about who we think we are.It is *a thought* we try to think apart from God. It is an error, a misperception, a fantasy which has nothing to do with truth. To the ego, the ego is God (T-13.II.6:3). It is a "will" in opposition to the Will of God. It is the part of us that likes being a separated individual.

The ego is nothing, and yet within the dream, it looks like everything. It is that which defines, interprets, projects, and judges. It is the thing that is always making up the world. You are—I am—we are—always making up the world. In truth, in reality, there is no ego. It is *just* an idea. According to the Course, the world was over long ago (T-28.I.1:6). The script is written. We can change our perception of the world but not the world, and we definitely cannot change Heaven. Accepting the truth means recognizing what already is. It means awakening from the dream.

> *The full awareness of the Atonement,*
> *then, is the recognition that the separation never occurred.*
> *The ego cannot prevail against this because it is an explicit*
> *statement that the ego never occurred.*
>
> T-6.II.10:7–8

**The devil is** also a *belief*, and, like the ego, does not exist. The mind can, however, make the belief in separation very real and very fearful. This *belief* is the devil (T-3.VIII.5:1). The devil is, therefore, roughly equivalent to the ego being other than our true Self.

**The body is** the ego's chosen home (T-23.I.3:3), a limitation in the dream, which, as Shakespeare said, "has its moment on the stage and then is seen no more." It is an image we have of ourselves, outside of ourselves. It is part of the mask, the persona, the disguise. Not knowing our True Identity, which extends far beyond the body, we think of ourselves as bodies. The body is neither good nor bad. Like the "world," the body is neutral. The only purpose of the body is the one given to it by the mind as a *teaching device* for learning how to awaken from the dream. Bodies are *temporary* limitations in form. A simple proof of the fact that we are not bodies is that within forty to fifty years the bodies of many of those who are reading these words will no longer exist. This in no way says anything about our eternity as spirit. Who is it that seems to possess the body? When anyone would ask the Indian Sage Ramana Maharshi (1879–1950) a question, he would often respond with, "Who wants to know?" Who is it behind the question?

**An Idol is** anything we place in front of God; anything that becomes a substitute for God. Idols are often unrecognized as we do not realize that we have made them as a replacement for God.

> *Your faith is placed in the most trivial and insane symbols;*
> *pills, money, "protective" clothing, influence, prestige,*
> *being liked, knowing the "right" people, and an endless list of forms*
> *of nothingness that you endow with magical powers.*

W-150: 1:3

An idol is an image of a brother or sister that we value more than what he or she is in truth. It is a wish, made tangible and real (T-29.VIII.3:2). It is a "belief." When the belief is withdrawn, the idol dies.

**A Miracle is** a correction introduced into false thinking (T-1.I.37). It is a change of mind which shifts perception from mindlessness to mindfulness. It is a dropping away of all of our defenses, all our hiding and our attack thoughts. It is the end of illusions. It is the undoing of the belief in sin, guilt, and fear. It is not a change in external circumstances. It is a correction of a misperception, a learning device, a lesson in truth, introduced into erroneous thinking. It is a putting-aside of false gods. It is the acceptance of the Atonement. The miracle does nothing. It undoes (T-28.I.1:1–2).

Our definition of terms continues in the next two chapters with a look at the basic *plot* in our story, the workings of the mind, and the basic dynamics of the ego.

# CHAPTER 5

# From Mindlessness to Mindfulness

## HOW THE MIND WORKS ACCORDING
## TO *A COURSE IN MIRACLES*

*Few appreciate the real power of the mind,*
*and no one remains fully aware of it all the time.*
*However, if you hope to spare yourself from fear there are some things*
*you must realize, and realize fully.*
*The mind is very powerful, and never loses its creative force.*
*It never sleeps. Every instant it is creating.*

T-2.VI.9:3–7

The Course makes repeated references to "choice and choosing" and "deciding and decision-making." Dr. Ken Wapnick repeatedly emphasizes the importance of the decision-maker. Living the Course means recognizing that we have made a decision for the ego; forgiving ourselves for having made that choice and then choosing to see things differently. Decision-making is as unknown in Heaven as is forgiveness because being of One Mind, there is no split; there is no division, and therefore, no decision (no judgment) to be made. In this sense we could say that, "freedom is just another word for nothing left to choose." Heaven is One-Mindedness. That Mind is of God and cannot be conflicted. In this moment, right now, I either know the peace of God or I do not. The next moment is the same, as is the next. The power of decision is our last remaining freedom (T-12.VII.9:1).

**Mind is** fundamental. Everything is in the Mind. There is no *thing* which is outside of the Mind. Mind is the activating or energizing agent of Spirit (C-1.1). There are two uses of "mind" in the Course. Capital "M" mind is the Mind of God equivalent with Love, Heaven, and Truth. Small "m" mind refers to the agent of choice in the world. We are free to believe whatever we want. We can choose to align our minds with the Holy Spirit, or with the small "m" mind—the ego, also referred to in the Course as wrong-mindedness. Miracle-mindedness means right-mindedness (T-2.V.3:1). We come to right-mindedness through the process of Atonement (the undoing of the ego). Living the Course therefore, means coming to right-mindedness. We need to be in our right mind in order to overcome guilt and separation. Right-mindedness is the willing-ness to turn things over. Right-mindedness is not the One-Mindedness of the Holy Spirit. It is, however, the state we must first achieve in order for One-Mindedness to be restored (T-4.II.10:1). We *elect* wrong-mindedness or right-mindedness. The only limit placed upon the mind, is to agree that it cannot serve two masters (Holy Spirit and ego).

> *No man can serve two masters: for either he will hate the one,*
> *and love the other; or else he will hold to the one, and despise the*
> *other. You cannot serve God and mammon.*
>
> MATTHEW 24:6

**Perception is** the process by which we give meaning and value to what we see, hear, or think. It is a reflection of our own thinking. Perception is *a mirror—not a fact* (W-304.1:3). God, Truth, and Love are changeless. Perception is *a process* of accepting and rejecting, shifting and changing. The ego limits perception to our brothers' and sisters' bodies and to the things of the world. It defines or concretizes the world. Perception is also a choice. Practicing the Course *purifies* perception by helping us remove the blocks (the teachings of fear) to an awareness of love's presence.

*For eyes and ears are senses without sense, and what they see and hear they but report. It is not they that hear and see, but you, who put together every jagged piece, each senseless scrap and shred of evidence, and make a witness to the world you want.*

T-5.V.6–7

**Knowledge,** which comes from our True Mind (the Mind of God), is eternal, impersonal, beyond subject and object, and the result of revelation (T-3.III.5:10). It is a direct contact with God that transcends time and abolishes fear. It is the experience of Oneness; the experience of Essence or Being. It is "illumination," and an insight into essence. It is stable, unchanging, and free of conflict.

**The miracle-minded are** those who, questioning the nature of dreaming (pain, suffering, and death), begin to practice steps leading to an awakening from the ego's dream. Miracle-mindedness means right-mindedness (T-2.V.3:1).

## How the Mind Works According to *A Course in Miracles*

1. **Life is Thought and God is Life** (T-14.IX.4:5). We are small "t" thought which "thought" that we could be separate from capital "T" Thought. We can imagine life without a body but we cannot imagine life without a mind. Life cannot be delimited by a plant, an animal, a human body, or any "thing." Life does not begin with the birth of a body. Life does not end with the death of a body. Life is a constant (eternal). The body is impermanence (finite).

> *When you made visible what is not true,*
> *what "is" true became invisible to you.*

> T-12.VIII.3:1

2. **Thought comes first.** God created thought. Before any "thing" (idea or object) can come into existence, it is first a thought. God did not create the external. God could not create that which is not of God. God did not create the ego. God did not create a meaningless world. The world we see is on the outside and of our own making.

> *In the beginning was the Word*
> *and the Word was with God, and the Word was God.*
> *The same was in the beginning with God.*
> *All things were made by him; and without him*
> *was not any thing made that was made.*
> *In him was life; and the life was the light of men.*
> *And the light shined in darkness;*
> *and the darkness comprehended it not.*

> JOHN 1:1–5

3. **Complete abstraction is the natural condition of the mind** (W-161.2:1). Love is abstract and cannot be defined, yet we all agree that there is something called love. God is abstract and cannot be defined yet most folks agree that there is a God.

> *The mind that taught itself to think specifically can no longer grasp abstraction in the sense that it is all-encompassing.*
> *We need to see a little, that we learn a lot.*

> W-166.4:7–8

Thinking specifically means thinking about the body, the world, and all the idols—all the external things the bodies' eyes see. Abstract thought applies to knowledge. Perception is always specific. Life seems to take form in bodies and therefore they appear as real, yet bodies are ephemeral and last only a moment in time and time itself is an illusion (T-20.VI.8:7–8). Divine Abstraction (God) takes joy in sharing (T-4.VI.5:4) that which is in creation.

*And why are you concerned about a speck in your brother's eye,*
*But consider not the beam in your own eye.*
*Or, how will you say to your brother.*
*Let me pull the mote out of your*
*eye and behold a beam blocks your own vision.*
*First remove the beam from your own eye;*
***and then you shall see clearly***
*how to cast out the mote from your brother's eye.*

MATTHEW 7:3–5 (BOLD MINE)

4. **Projection makes perception.** This simple, three-word sentence, which appears twice in the Course is straightforward, profound, and yet, not easily understood (accepted) because we are so persistently engaged in projection that we do not see that we are projecting. We do not realize that we are making up the world we see. We see the world as insane and we do not see that we are "the image maker." The purpose of all seeing is to show us what we wish to see and all hearing brings to mind the sounds we expect to hear (W-161.2.3:5–6).

According to the Heisenberg Principle in physics, it is impossible for the perceiver not to affect the object perceived. The preamble to UNESCO begins with the phrase, "Wars begin in the minds of men." If wars begin in the minds of men then wars also end in the minds of men. Everything is a projection—an assertion—from the first cry of the infant coming out of the womb, onward. "Projection makes perception and perception means interpretation" (T-3.I.1:6). We superimpose our interpretations on the world, thus, believing that what we see is reality.

*The ego analyzes; the Holy Spirit accepts.*

T-11.V.13:1

The basic difference between the ordinary ego mind which includes most all of our thinking most all of the time, and miracle-mindedness is that the ordinary ego mind is a *projector*. Miracle-mindedness is "receptive" rather than "projective." It simply sees. It simply is. In the Holy Instant, when time stops its ceaseless tides, we see truly. Miracle-mindedness sees without the contaminations of the ego—without projecting anything onto the world. We cannot be projective and receptive at the same time.

5.  **The ultimate purpose of projection is always to get rid of guilt** (T-13.II.1:1). If we did not feel guilty we would not project. Guilt stands in the way of our remembering God, so we try to get rid of it by projecting it outward.

6.  **Ideas leave not their source.** We never left home (Heaven) because the impossible cannot happen. It is precisely because ideas do not leave their source that I am not a body. I am a mind. Seeing how I am a mind, the Inner Teacher (Holy Spirit) is going to get through at the level it can get though and that is the level of mind. As ideas do not leave their source, we cannot be separate from God. The idea of God has never left the Mind that thought it, which is why, in order to be whole, I must give my whole mind back to God. In the same way, the idea of guilt does not leave its starting place in the mind. The idea of separation has never left the

mind that thought it. For this reason, I am never angry at someone else. I am always angry at myself.

*Since the Holy Spirit is in your mind, your mind can also believe only what is true. The Holy Spirit can speak only for this, because He speaks for God. He tells you to return your whole mind to God, because it has never left Him.*

T-6.II.10:3–5

When I was eighteen years old, I listened to a cassette tape by Earl Nightingale called *The Greatest Secret in the World.* According to Nightingale, the greatest secret in the world was that "we become what we think about." Or, we are what we think about. What seems to be external is not outside the mind. What I see is witness to my thoughts. The world I perceive is a representation of my mind; *the outside picture of an inward condition.* Or, as someone once said, "The universe constantly rearranges itself to accommodate my interpretation of reality." Workbook Lesson 35 is *My mind is part of God's. I am very holy.* This is obviously not the way we see ourselves. It is, however the way things are in truth. Perception can be changed; the object of perception cannot be changed. Our thoughts change our lives. Get it and you will get it!

*Do not forget that your will has power over all fantasies and dreams. Trust it to see you through, and carry you beyond them all.*

W-RII.IN.4

7. **The thoughts "we think we think" are not our real thoughts** (W-45:1-2). Life is thought. Life is God. Our *real thoughts* are those thoughts we think in line with the Mind of God. When we do not think like God we are not really

thinking (T-5.V.6:12). All thought of aloneness, isolation, pain, guilt, and fear are not real (eternal). All thoughts which stand outside of the Mind of God are *fantasies, wishes, illusion,* or *dreams.* All of our "secret thoughts," things we think we cannot share, are equally unreal. Like all dreams, they last a moment and then they disappear. They are distortions of reality. They are make-believe or made up. When someone alters their appearance by decorating their face, we call it makeup. We make up a world. Our fantasies, dreams, and illusions are not true; and, there is a place inside us which knows these thoughts are temporal not eternal, and therefore, not real. And yet . . .

*Your Self retains Its Thoughts,*
*and they remain within your mind and in the Mind of God.*

W-96.7:1

8. **There are no neutral thoughts.** Our thoughts are fearful or loving but never neutral. There are no idle thoughts. All thinking produces form at some level (T-2.VI.9:13). This is true both within the dream world (this world) and the real world (Heaven). Within the context of "this world" my thoughts create a temporal, artificial, and fearful world.

9. **The real world is a state in which there is no good and evil.** Dutch philosopher Benedict de Spinoza (1632–1677) observed that "If men were born free, they would so long as they remained free, form no conception of good and evil." Although it is not so in this world (in illusion), in "reality" there is no division, thus again, there is no decision. Knowledge never involves comparison (T-4.II.11:12).

*The real world can actually be perceived.*
*All that is necessary is a willingness to perceive nothing else.*
*For if you perceive both good and evil,*
*you are accepting both the false and the true*
*and making no distinction between them.*

T-11.VII.2:6–8

10. **Our only problem is our belief in separation!** There is
   only one solution: the acceptance of Atonement (undoing of
   the ego) which means that the separation never happened.
   It just "looks like" it did. The separation actually never
   occurred. It was (is) all a dream. We come to this memory
   through the process of forgiveness—by letting the world
   be what it is without projecting onto it. When we stop
   projecting our perception, we experience Oneness. Only
   then do we experience true empathy, only then can we be
   truly helpful.

   *Belief that there is another way of perceiving is the loftiest idea*
   *of which ego thinking is capable. That is because it contains*
   *a hint of recognition that the ego is not the Self.*

   T-4.II.4:10–11

11. **There are no private thoughts.** Minds are joined and only
   minds communicate (T-7.V.2:1). One brother is all brothers
   and every mind contains all minds (W-161.4:1–2). Just as
   the idea of separation has to be shared before there can be
   separation; as oneness is shared, so is there only oneness.
   Joy, peace, oneness, and love come in an integrated willingness to share and promote the mind's natural impulse to
   respond as one (T-5.in.1.6). Our only completely meaningful

relationship is with God who is Oneness. We know the
Oneness of God as we literally share that oneness with every
other mind.

12. **Only minds communicate** (T-2.V.2:1), and minds do not
    need bodies to communicate. The body can only do what
    the mind directs it to do. While the body, in service to
    the ego, can certainly hurt other bodies; minds cannot
    hurt. We're all familiar with the truth in the old children's
    adage, "Sticks and stones may break my bones but words
    can never hurt me." To communicate is to join. To attack
    is to separate. Although minds can communicate, they
    can communicate only in love. Everything else is a form of
    separation or miscommunication.

13. **We are never alone in experiencing the effects of our
    seeing** (Lesson 18). I can call upon my loving thoughts
    which share everything with everyone. As thoughts of
    separation disconnect me from others, my real thoughts
    awaken real thoughts in others (W-54.3:6). Just as hiding
    makes us miserable, nothing is more delightful than shar-
    ing. Joy comes in sharing. This is love. God is Love.

14. **Everything I say, do, or think teaches the universe.** We
    are all, at all times, students and teachers. We teach the
    Course by living the Course.

> *If the center of the thought system is true,*
> *only truth extends from it.*
> *But if a lie is at its center, only deception proceeds from it.*

T-6.V.B.1:11

15. **All false systems of belief fail.** The totalitarian system
    of communism failed because it was a totalitarian system.

We cannot be made equal by taking away freedom. Many years ago, I became aware of what *seemed* to be *A Course in Miracles* cult, formed around a charismatic leader. Concerned about this possible misinterpretation of the Course, I called Ken Wapnick. Ken's response was to quote a piece of scripture which said, "If this be of God there is nothing you can do to stop it, and if it is not of God, it will come to naught." A study of history shows—the ego always implodes. When it does, truth automatically comes to the fore.

16. **I am determined to see.** Love can replace fear. Laughter can replace tears. Abundance can replace loss. It is not only possible for my will and the Will of God to be One, it is the only way—the only truth there is.

**Who is in charge of the mind?** The Course says that *you* (the decision-maker) are in charge of the journey, the Sonship, the process of Atonement, the second coming, the Kingdom, and the universe. Engaging in the process of purification, undoing the ego and aligning my mind with the Mind of God, I know these statements to be true.

> *When you let your mind be drawn to bodily concerns,*
> *to things you buy, to eminence as valued by the world,*
> *you ask for sorrow, not for happiness.*

W-133.2:2

Who is it that *lets the mind be drawn*; and, when I see that I am letting the mind be drawn down a path of miscreation, can I refocus the mind so that I can get the results that I want truly and not simply something of the world? Into whose service do I place the mind? And, who is the "I" that does the placing? We never stop being decision-makers. We can give the mind into the service of the One who can lead us to our true Home and not simply turn it over to mindlessness—a place where we wander around lost in a dreaming of the world.

*Your mind cannot be stopped in this unless you choose to stop it.*

W-44.7:3

## Stop It!

There is a television clip with comedian Bob Newhart from the 1980s, where Bob plays the part of a psychiatrist. A woman comes into his office for counseling and Bob tells her that the consultation will be five dollars in advance and she says, "Five dollars in advance, why five dollars?" He says, "I charge one dollar per minute and this will only take five minutes." So, she says, "very well," and she gives him five dollars. He then says, "How can I help you?" She says, "I am afraid of being buried alive in a box." He says, "Well, Stop That!" She says, "You mean I should just stop thinking about that?" He says, "Yes, Stop It!" Then she says she has another problem. He asks her what it is and she says she lets men take advantage of her and he says, "Well, Stop It!" Correction is not, of course, always so instantaneous but the principle remains the same. Not until I realize that I have a choice and I decide to follow the Voice for God, can I indeed make that decision.

## When Judgment Ceases, Healing Occurs

Judgment dissipates as we change the way we look at things. Vigilance (watching our thoughts) requires effort until it does not require any effort. We've been judging all our lives and we don't just stop judgment. Watch what is going on without making judgments about what is going on. Not judging does not mean not making simple judgments or what might be called discernments. "Am I having eggs or oatmeal for breakfast?" or "What am I going to wear?" What we're wearing doesn't make much difference unless we're into power dressing or sexy dressing, in which case, we are trying to manipulate the universe. Dress the way regular people do. Dress to be comfortable.

What we're watching for is projection, condemnation, criticism, attack, and blame. If I condemn a brother, I condemn someone that God condemns not. Condemnation is not of God. To condemn my brother, is to place a crown of thorns upon my own head. And to nail myself to a cross. Try fasting from judging. See it and stop it. See it and stop it. The ego always speaks first (T-5.VI.3:5). We're trying to retrain the mind so think more than twice before speaking. Look at the world without adding anything to it. Just see it as it. Let it be what it is. The world has always been the domain of the ego. It always will be. It is something which is happening in time. For this reason, there will never be a solution to terrorism—in this world. In Heaven, there is no such thing as terrorism. There could not be. You are timeless and from a position of timelessness you can see it—being thus, above the battlefield. I am no better or any worse than anyone else. My needs are no more important than anyone else's and I recognize my inherent Oneness with all things. Seeing this is truly loving.

A Holy Instant is any moment in which by not judging I do not see myself as separate. Psychotherapy works when the therapist does not judge his client. There are, of course, differences in form but not in content. God literally has no favorite sons, no favorite daughters. As my friend, Reverend Sara Emrie says it, "Why don't we just say things the way they are? We are One."

*Miracles are thoughts.*
*Thoughts can represent the lower or bodily level of experience,*
*or the higher or spiritual level of experience.*
*One makes the physical, and the other creates the spiritual.*

PRINCIPLE NUMBER 12 OF THE 50 MIRACLES PRINCIPLES, T-1.I.12

## Putting it in Hyper-Drive

What do we mean by taking things to a higher or spiritual level? In the original Star Wars trilogy, our hero, Hans Solo (played by Harrison Ford) and his companions are able to escape Darth Vader and the Evil Empire by putting their spacecraft, the Millennium Falcon, into hyper-drive, thus taking it to another dimension. In the same way, when we move from the ego mind (mindlessness) to the higher mind (mindfulness), we go to a higher dimension outside of time and space and our ordinary ways of thinking, we switch from ego to spirit, from eyes of fear to eyes of love, from being projective to being receptive.

After Dr. Bill Thetford retired, when someone asked him what he was doing, he would say that he was practicing forgiveness. Until I have brought my mind completely in line with the Mind of God, I keep asking, "Is this a truly loving thought or am I projecting?" If it is coming from guilt or fear; if it is some place I am hiding; if it is coming out of anger; if it is a form of vengeance; I can be sure that it is not true and I need to take it to a higher level. I need another way of seeing. The last lesson in *A Course in Miracles* is repeated in Lessons 361–365.

> *This holy instant would I give to You*
> *Be You in Charge. For I would follow You,*
> *Certain that Your direction gives me peace.*

WORKBOOK LESSONS 361–365

======

# CHAPTER 6

# The Dynamics of the Ego

## Demythologizing Adam and Eve

*The Garden of Eden, or the pre-separation condition, was a state of mind in which nothing was needed. When Adam listened to the "lies of the serpent," all he heard was untruth. You do not have to continue to believe what is not true unless you choose to do so.*

T-2.I.3:1–3

## Becoming Disillusioned—How Did the Ego Get Started?

No matter how much it may appear to be otherwise—we are not an ego and we are not a body. Being a belief or a dream, the ego never got started but—it sure looks like it did! The deeper question is not how did the ego get started but—why do we perpetuate it? Why can't we stop it? Why can't we let it go? Being immersed in the ego is like not being able to see the forest for the trees. How do we let go of an illusion, if we do not know that we are caught in one? After all, the main quality of an illusion is that it is an illusion.

In the third chapter of the book of Genesis, in the beginning of the Bible, we find the most fundamental myth of the Western World, basic to Judaism, Christianity, and Islam. This myth explains the origin and persistence of the ego. Adam (man) and Eve (woman) are created in a state of innocent, unself-consciousness. Adam bites into the fruit of the knowledge of good and evil and suddenly, "his eyes are opened." Duality comes into the mind and Adam thinks it possible to think a thought outside of the mind of God. Man is now seemingly cast out of Heaven (Oneness) and thrown into hell (Duality). Trying to live in duality is an ambiguity.

Adam and Eve, man, woman, you, me, us—*we* decided that it was possible to live outside of the Mind of God. This thought is a kind of curse, a kind of temporal, but not eternal, damnation. It is not possible to be separated from God (Eternity). In time, however, in the past several million years or more, several billion of us have been "trying" to think a thought outside of the Mind of God. We listen not to the Voice for God; we listen instead to a voice that tells us preposterous things. It says it's okay to be selfish; it's okay to be angry; it's okay to look for fault and find the error. It's okay to attack. We can even, in righteousness, go to war and kill our brothers and sisters with complete justification. Hurting someone else, however, is never a joyful experience. We cannot inflict pain upon another without inflicting it upon ourselves.

> *Into eternity, where all is one, there crept a tiny, mad idea,*
> *at which the Son of God remembered not to laugh.*

T-27.VIII.6:2

We might think of the "big bang" as the first projection; the first formation of form out of formlessness; the first thought of individuality that "thought" to separate itself from Thought (God). Before the "big bang" there was no division, no separation, no splintering off of the mind; and, there was no time. The ego lives in time, in history, in a story. The magnitude of this one thought (projection/error) is so vast that a world of unreality emerges from it. Like a mirror which is dropped and shatters, a kind of fractal splintering off of consciousness occurs, breaking repeatedly into trillions upon trillions of individual pieces of non-reality.

Shame and guilt have come into the mind. Something has happened that was not supposed to happen. We now have self and other, good and bad, pretty and ugly, and all of it requires judgment. Defenses of all sorts suddenly became necessary. We have judgment; we have separation and division; we do not have the whole; we do not have vastness; we do not have the infinite. We have instead the concrete, the physical, the material, the mundane, and the limited. (There is no mention of an apple in the book of Genesis. I have sometimes joked that the fabled apple might have been a mushroom that is some kind of psychotropic.)

> *Adam was but human—this explains it all.*
> *He did not want the apple for the apple's sake;*
> *he wanted it only because it was forbidden.*
> *The mistake was in not forbidding the serpent;*
> *then he would have eaten the serpent.*
>
> AMERICAN AUTHOR, MARK TWAIN (1835–1910)

## Ego Defense Mechanisms

Let's leave Adam in the bushes for a moment and talk about modern psychology. Although Eastern philosophy has for centuries been onto the ego, it was not until the development of German Idealistic philosophy of the eighteenth and nineteenth centuries that the role of the ego was more clearly seen in the West. German philosopher J.G. Fichte (1762–1814) said that seeing how the ego was the determiner of the world we see, shouldn't the ego be the primary thing that philosophy studies? It is Austrian psychiatrist Sigmund Freud (1856–1939), however, who explains in depth the variety of ego defense mechanisms available for us. Thanks to Freud; his daughter, Anna Freud; Carl Jung; and the founders of modern depth psychology, we now have more clarity about the origin, structure, and evolution of the mechanisms of the ego. Freud was an atheist; and, while he understood the ego very well, he thought the mind was limited to the brain. He did not take the Eastern philosophical position that the ego was unreal. He was studying, after all, something which looked very real. He thought that we were stuck with the ego—damned with it if you will. There was simply no way out. What the Course is saying, what mystical philosophy has always said is—there is a way out.

> *The "dynamics" of the ego will be our lesson for a while, for we*
> *must look first at this to see beyond it, since you have made it real.*
> *We will undo this error quietly together,*
> *and then look beyond it to truth.*

T-11.V.1:5–6

**Defenses are** the mechanisms we use to protect ourselves from what we perceive as threats from the outside world. They are the ways we try to build up and protect our own world. They are the means by which we promote separation. Defenses are insane thoughts simply because they are broken off from the whole. They are "secret, magic wands" we wave when truth appears to threaten what we believe about ourselves. They are "foolish guardians of mad illusions" (M-4.VI.1). The primary defenses are denial and projection.

> *Consider what the ego wants defenses for.*
> *Always to justify what goes against the truth,*
> *flies in the face of reason and makes no sense.*

T-25.II.5:1–2

*Defenses are the costliest of all the prices*
*which the ego would exact.*

W-153.4:1

**Denial is** the first line of defense—lie, hide, don't look, go unconscious, run away, knock ourselves out with alcohol or a drug, etc. While each of the defenses takes on a variety of forms, three of the most obvious forms of denial are: 1. hiding or lying; 2. dissociation; and, 3. addictive behaviors. There are obvious overlaps. For example, we lie about, hide, or deny addictive behaviors. Lying is a form of hiding. What is the first thing that Adam does after "his eyes are opened" and he is able to distinguish between "good and evil"? He hides in the bushes. According to the Bible, God goes looking for Adam "in the cool of the day." God finds Adam in the bushes, and He says, "Why are you hiding?" Adam had never hidden from God before. There would have been no need for it. Now things have changed and Adam says, "Because I was naked." And God says, "Who told you that you were naked?" (Genesis 3:11) Where did this idea of naked come from? Where there was simply being, there is now a body, a past, a future, and a story.

*And you have done a stranger thing than you yet realize.*
*You have displaced your guilt to your body from your mind.*

T-18.VI.2:4

The experience of shame or guilt—dirty, stinky, awful guilt has come into the mind. Adam has been exposed. He has a body and his guilt is related not just to any body, but a naked body. It also has something to do with sex, so Adam must now "hide his shame."

Lying is a primary defense we learn as children. When we get into a little bit of trouble and need to protect ourselves—we just tell a lie. After all, who is going to know? The problem is, of course, that someone knows—"we" know.

This deepens our experience of guilt, because we have separated ourselves from the one we have lied to, and thus, from the whole or Oneness; and, our guilt automatically produces a fear of punishment. The first person you probably lied to (which produced an experience of guilt and separation) was your mother. It probably happened a little bit like this: Mother walked into your room, saw a mess and said, "What happened here?" And you said: "I don't know!" Or, we might quickly go to projection: "I think the dog did it."

> *. . . projection, occurs when you believe that some emptiness*
> *or lack exists in you, and that you can fill it*
> *with your own ideas instead of truth.*

> T-2.I.1:7

While our first choice is often to run away, hide, or dissociate, the ego's major choice for defense is attack or projection. God presses Adam to tell Him a little more about what has happened. Adam goes to the second line of defense and comes up with Eve. (What other choice did he have?) "Eve gave me this fruit and I did eat thereof." God goes to Eve and says, "Look Eve, what happened?" Eve immediately goes to the second line of defense and says, "The serpent did beguile (trick) me, and I did eat thereof."

**Projection is** a more obvious form of defense. Indeed the mind can be very busily engaged in projection. To project means to "hurl out" or to "throw away." Projection reinforces the belief in separation. When we project, we make ourselves different from and more important than that onto which we project; thereby, reinforcing our belief in separation. The purpose of projection is to get rid of guilt.

> *Anger always involves projection of separation,*
> *which must ultimately be accepted as one's own*
> *responsibility, rather than being blamed on others.*

> T-6.IN.1:2

**Anger and attack** are the primary ways in which we project. To the extent to which we value guilt, we believe that attack is justified (T-25.III.1). The ego loves to be right. The Course asks us, however, if we would rather be right or happy (T-29.VIII.1:9)? Anger is the means by which we refuse to acknowledge our own guilt and our own responsibility. We then say, "The problem is not in me—it's in you," and that makes me angry and gives me the right to attack you. What I attack in you is the sin I see inside me; otherwise, I could not attack.

A student asked Zen Master Bankei, "How can I cure my terrible temper?" "Show it to me," demanded Bankei. "I can't just show it to you like that because it comes on unexpectedly," explained the student. Bankei replied, "Then it is not your true nature. If it were, it would be with you at all times." Attack cannot occur without judgment; and "anger is never justified" (T-30.VI.1:1). The word is *never*, not *sometimes*. The ego would love it if the Course said that anger was *sometimes justified.* Then we could have debates about the times it was and the times it is not justified. This does not mean we should never get angry; it just means I have slipped into fear, something has gone wrong with my thinking, and I need another way to look at things.

## The Defense of Atonement

The Atonement is correction or undoing. It is the only defense the ego did not make (T-2.II.4:1). It is God's plan (curriculum) for salvation through forgiveness (letting go of that which we are projecting or are holding on to). Atonement is a practical process for releasing the ego's belief in separation. It is, in fact, the awareness that the separation never happened. It cannot be used destructively. It cannot fail. It can, however, be refused.

If I have a gold chain, or maybe a headset cord which has become tangled with knots and I have to undo the mess, I *reverse* the process by which the knots occurred. The undoing may occur quickly; or, if the knots are tight and *seem* complicated, it may be necessary to work for a long time on just one little section and then suddenly when that section is undone, a whole length comes out. If I succeed in undoing all the knots in a gold chain and I get down to the end, I find there is nothing there. So it is in my mind. There is nothing there unless we think that there is something there. As Shakespeare's Hamlet says it, "Nothing is good or bad but thinking makes it so." In like manner, as the ego is undone, we find there was nothing there to start with. The ego really is nothing. It never was anything. How can nothing become something? For this reason, there is nothing to forgive unless "we think" there is. Take jealously, for example. Jealously can only occur if I think that something has been taken away from me—that I have been deprived of love. Some little "kinky" thing happened and I let it become a knot in my thinking.

A student in one of our Course meetings brought the following illustration to the group. His daughter was getting married. He was now divorced from his daughter's mom. She had now remarried and so had he. At the wedding, no one picked up the microphone to acknowledge him as the father of the bride. He got so upset that he left the wedding. He got into his car and started to drive. He was soon insane with anger and rage. And then a miracle happened. He realized what he was doing. He had slipped into a temporary state of insanity. He reversed his thinking. It did not matter if he was recognized as the father of the bride or not—or, it mattered only in his egoist mind and he could let that go. What mattered was the love he felt for his daughter. He turned the car around, went back to the wedding, and apologized to his daughter for having left. Love prevailed. Forgiveness prevailed. He had a dance with his daughter and all was well.

> *The sole responsibility of God's teacher is to accept the Atonement for himself. Atonement means correction, or the undoing of errors.*

*When this has been accomplished, the teacher of God becomes*
*a miracle worker by definition. His sins have been forgiven him,*
*and he no longer condemns himself.*
*How can he then condemn anyone?*
*And who is there whom his forgiveness can fail to heal?*

M-18.4:5–10

## Reversing Our Thinking

B y offering complete forgiveness to everyone, including ourselves, we undo guilt. Miracles are part of a chain of undoing. We may think of what happened with Adam and Eve as a reversal in thinking. The natural *miraculous* state of mind was lost and an artificial, though seemingly very real, perspective was adopted. What is needed then is a reversal in thinking in order to bring us back home to God.

*If I had a world of my own,*
*everything would be nonsense.*
*Nothing would be what it is*
*because everything would be what it isn't.*
*And contrary-wise; what it is it wouldn't be,*
*and what it wouldn't be, it would. You see?*

ALICE IN *ALICE IN WONDERLAND*

An Experimental psychologist, G. M. Stratton, made glasses for himself in which the world was inverted upside-down and backward. He wore the glasses constantly and eventually learned to live in a contrary-wise upside-down, backward world. He could write, eat, dress—literally do everything upside-down and backward. He even got to the point where he forgot that he was living in an upside-down, backward world. When he took the glasses off, the world was again, of course, inverted and backward and he had to learn how to live in this world all over again.

*What we are familiar with we cease to see.*

FRENCH AUTHOR, ANAÏS NIN (1903–1977)

It does not occur to us that we are seeing ourselves backward when we look into a mirror, unless we're wearing a name badge. Then it is clear something is amiss. Either everything is backward or our perception is backward. In a similar way, the ego does a psychological inversion of reality that is completely backward, but we don't see it. We think that this world is real and Heaven is a fantasy. It's the other way around. Heaven is reality and the world is a dream.

*Complexity is of the ego, and is nothing more than the ego's attempt to obscure the obvious.*

T-15.IV.6:2

Lesson 11 from the Workbook, "My meaningless thoughts are showing me a meaningless world," is a beginning step in the reversal of our thinking process. It seems as if the world determines what we perceive. It's the other way around—our thoughts determine the world we perceive.

*It would be so nice if something would make sense for a change.*

ALICE IN *ALICE IN WONDERLAND*

A reversal in thinking is called for as it is, for example, in understanding forgiveness. (As we forgive so are we forgiven.) The ego does not understand forgiveness; and, thus, twists it into something it is not. Making the other wrong and then forgiving them for our projection is backward thinking. We resist the Atonement and the process of the Course as we are blinded by our own reflection. We've been looking at the world so long "through a glass darkly" that all we see is the ego's reflection.

*Denial of error is a strong defense of truth, but denial of truth results in miscreation, the projections of the ego.*

T-2.II.2:5

## Extension, the Correct Form of Projection

Fortunately for every defense of the ego, the Holy Spirit has an alternative defense which cannot harm. In fact, it can only heal. The positive use of denial means that we deny the denial of truth and we assert that only the truth can be true. Only Heaven is true. A dream is never reality. What we deny is the ego's whole thought system and its seeming truth. We deny the belief that we can be hurt by error. Jesus goes to the cross without attacking those who have misperceived, and therefore, persecuted him. He does not amplify or make the error real. The Course calls upon us to deny any belief that error can hurt us.

*When a child is helped to translate his "ghost" into a curtain, his "monster" into a shadow, and his "dragon" into a dream he is no longer afraid, and laughs happily at his own fear.*

T-11.VIII.13:3

While the ego projects to exclude, and therefore, to deceive the Holy Spirit, the extension of love sees only oneness. As the Course expresses it, "The great peace of the Kingdom shines in your mind forever, but it must shine outward to make you aware of it" (T-6.II.2:8). As I extend love, so do I come to know what love is. The ego is depression and the more I am trapped, or caught, or locked within my own mind, the greater is my isolation and despair. Depression "is" isolation and the inescapable consequence of separation.

> *God, Who encompasses all being,*
> *created beings who have everything*
> *individually, but who want to share it to increase their joy.*
> *Nothing real can be increased except by sharing.*
> *That is why God created you.*
> *Divine Abstraction takes joy in sharing.*

T-4.VIII.5:1–2

===

# CHAPTER 7

# The Undoing of Guilt

## OUR WAY OUT OF FEAR

*What else but sin could be the source of guilt,*
*demanding punishment and suffering?*
*And what but sin could be the source of fear,*
*obscuring God's creation;*
*giving love the attributes of fear and of attack?*

W-259.1:4–5

The moment Adam's eyes are opened and he distinguishes between good and evil, guilt comes into the mind. Now there are two possibilities: one right, one wrong. Now there is division. There is separation. There is judgment. There is guilt. Never wholly present, sin is always a judgment about a past event. It may have been five minutes ago or five thousand years ago. It is still past. Guilt is self-accusation. It is my experience in the moment and fear is my dread of possible punishment. If I feel guilty, it means *I have sinned* and if I have sinned that means that I now feel separate from God—from wholeness. I am isolated and alone and fearful that God will reprimand me for what I have done.

As the mind is split, there are two possible memories for the mind. I can wallow in my ego's past, a place of error and wrong decisions, and thus, a place of guilt, separation, and division. Or, I can return my mind to the memory of the truth of Being in God, a place in which there is no division or separation, only love, only God. Memory is selective. If we did not want the ego, if we did not desire its effect, if we did not want to be separate from God, we would not wander into guilt. There is really one problem and that is the mind's decision for separation, division, individuality, aloneness, and isolation. The decision for separation is the bringer of guilt.

> *The world but demonstrates an ancient truth;*
> *you will believe that others do to you*
> *exactly what you think you did to them.*
> *But once deluded into blaming them*
> *you will not see the cause of what*
> *they do, because you "want" the guilt to rest on them.*
> *How childish is the petulant device to keep your innocence*
> *by pushing guilt outside yourself, but never letting go!*

T-27.VIII.8:1–3

## The Miracle Reverses Projection

Seeing that *projection makes perception*, we place ourselves in a position where we can choose once again—this time from a position of Mindfulness (sanity) instead of mindlessness (insanity). The insanity is that I am choosing the ego when I could be choosing peace instead. I do not try to change the world. I rather change my mind about the world. Mindlessness sees sin. Mindfulness sees oneness. We see guilt's shadow all around us and we don't realize that it is inside. It's in my own mind and if I see it in a brother then I am projecting that guilt outward from my mind, onto my brother. Thus it is when I condemn my brother that I condemn myself, and I see us both in hell. If I release (forgive) my brother, we are both set free.

*Choose once again if you would take your place among the saviors*
*of the world, or would remain in hell, and hold your brothers there.*

T-31.VIII.1:5

*If on my brothers sins I dwell.*
*I seek to send us both to hell.*
*If I forgive, I am set free*
*and again I know eternity.*

**Sin is the** *belief* in separation or "the idea of evil" (T-19.III.5:1). It is a lack of love. When we read the word *sin* in the Course, we can use the word *separation*. When we read *separation*, we can use the word *sin*. Sin is the belief that it is possible to do something against God. A man went to church without his wife. When he returned home, she asked him what the preacher talked about. He said, "Sin." "Well," said the wife, "what did he have to say about it?" "He's against it," said the husband. Traditional Christianity has always been against sin. Sin means taking the ego seriously. Sin is precious to the ego, so much so that the ego seeks out sin to provide testimony to its reality. The word *sin* (*hamartia*), as Jesus uses it in the New Testament, means "missing the mark," or "missing the point." Being centered means being in focus. Being egocentric, we place our focus on who we think we are rather than who we are in truth.

*Sin is a strictly individual perception,*
*seen in the other yet believed by each to be within himself.*

T-19.III.1:6

The more easily I see sin in myself, the more it is projected outward; the more real it seems; the more power it also seems to have over me. "There is," the ego says, "plenty of sin"—just look around. Sin is sacred to the ego. It is, in fact, the most "holy" concept in the ego's system (T-19. II.4:2). Believing in sin, good and bad, and right and wrong, makes judgment necessary.

> *Guilt is the psychological experience of the belief*
> *in sin and can be defined as the total of all our*
> *negative thoughts, feelings and beliefs about ourselves.*

DR. KENNETH AND GLORIA WAPNICK, IN *AWAKEN FROM THE DREAM*

**Guilt is** the belief we have sinned. It is the preserver of time. It is any negative thought we have about ourselves. It is a painful feeling, emotion, or thought which arises when we believe we have hurt the whole or oneness including ourselves. Guilt manifests as contempt of self, incompleteness, failure, indifference, despair, depression, and loneliness. It is the "idea" that we can think apart from God. Without the ego, there would be no guilt. Without guilt, there would be no ego. If I am feeling guilty, I can be sure that the ego is in charge because only the ego can feel guilty (T-4. IV.5:5). The purpose of the ego is to keep us guilty. Guilt is an invention of my own mind which means that guilt and salvation are in the same place. Guilt is a "decision" within my mind. Not being guilty means not being invested in the ego.

> *Guilt is a sure sign that your thinking is unnatural.*
> *Unnatural thinking will always be attended with guilt,*
> *because it is the belief in sin.*

T-5.V.4:8–9

## Unconscious Guilt

My mother, Milly, passed on Christmas Day 2001, at the age of eighty-five. We were talking on the phone one day when she was about eighty years old, and she said she felt guilty. I said, "About what, momma?" She was, as far as I knew, the embodiment of innocence and the most loving person I had ever known. She said, "I don't know. It's just a feeling." I think mother's guilt was the anxiety everyone feels about the wrongness of feeling separated, and therefore ego-driven. There is no one that has not struggled, or is not now struggling, with guilt. We have all lied, been thoughtless, and condemning of others. We have each been selfish, pushy, arrogant, and rude. We have lost our tempers and cheated at a game and on our taxes; thereby, experiencing separation from the one we cheated on or lied to. We do things "in secret" and pray that no one will find out. We have forgotten who we are. We have misidentified ourselves as abandoned, unloved, unlovable, alone, and vulnerable; and, we see each other as antagonists, adversaries, and enemies.

> *When you maintain that you are guilty but the source*
> *of your guilt lies in the past, you are not looking inward.*
> *The past is not "in" you.*

T-13.X.4:1-2

Guilt is self attack and it is *always* insane. To get rid of it, we project it out and when we project it, we cannot then be free of it. Guilt never finds its home in the present. It is always about the past. While there is no eternal hell, the experience of guilt in the now moment is hellish. It keeps me from awareness of wholeness and Heaven. Guilt comes in relationship to our bodies, each other, and time. It is, after all, through the body that I "experience" separation from other bodies. Guilt often arises around indulgence of the body in eating, illness, smoking, sexuality, alcohol, and drugs, to name a few.

> *It is essential that error be not confused with sin,*
> *and it is this distinction that makes salvation possible.*
> *For error can be corrected, and the wrong made right.*
> *But sin, were it possible, would be irreversible.*

> T-19.II.1:1–2

## Mistakes and Misperception

If it really was possible to be separated from God, then sin would be real. It is precisely because sin is an illusion that it is not real. It is actually impossible to be separated from God. We just think that we can be and that gives birth to "the dream of sin" (W-193.5:4). Sin is not to be confused with error. Error or mistaken perception calls for correction. A young woman went to see her priest. "Father," she said, "you must forgive me for I have sinned." "My goodness," said the priest, "what is your sin?" "Well," she said, "I have committed the sin of vanity." "How is that, dear?" asked the priest. "Every day," she answered, "I go and stand in front of the mirror and say, you are so beautiful. You are absolutely gorgeous." "Oh my goodness," said the priest, "That is not a sin. It's just a mistake."

Sin is not real. Though we may be much mistaken, we cannot transgress against God. Our Father has only love for us. Love does not condemn. Love cannot be hurt. The Course says that God is lonely without us. Lonely should be understood metaphorically. *We* are incomplete without God. We are lonely without Him. God does not hate us and he does not punish us. That does not mean we can do any hateful thing we want. If we do, "we" suffer. We suffer because selfishness is suffering.

In the parable of the Prodigal Son, the Father says nothing about where the son went, what he did, or the level of illusion that he got caught in. We all come into the world and then get caught in a variety of illusions. Where he went, what he did, the level of illusion *we* get caught in does not matter. The only thing which matters is that we wake up and come Home again. Children are not punished because they sleep and while they sleep they have bad dreams.

> *Son of God, you have not sinned,*
> *but you have been much mistaken.*
> *Yet this can be corrected and God will help you,*
> *knowing that you could not sin against Him.*

T-10.V.6:1–2

God has not condemned us. Neither need we condemn ourselves. The past was what it was and the best I can do with it is not drag it into the present. The present is where Heaven is. The present is where oneness is. If guilt is in my own mind then salvation is there as well. As long as the problem is out there, I don't have to look inside. My *seeing* your sin is proof that "I am right and you're wrong." I have a book with illustrations for use in sermons by Christian ministers. It defines sin as "that abominable thing that God hates." If God is Love, can God hate? Mistakes can be forgiven; error can be corrected; the wrong can be made right.

**Fear is** a witness to separation and an expectation of punishment (pain) (T-4.I.10:2). Fear is a synonym for ego. Love is a synonym for God. The last sentence of the first paragraph of the Introduction to the Course says, "The opposite of love is fear, but what is all-encompassing can have no opposite." There is no opposite to God, which is why what is not of God, what is not of Love—does not exist. Think of a time when you were most fearful and you can probably see that you were very much in ego.

Think of a time when joy and love filled your heart and you see that you also felt close to God.

> *There is no time, no place, no state where God is absent.*
> *There is nothing to be feared.*
> *There is no way in which a gap could be*
> *conceived of in the Wholeness that is His.*

T-29.I.2-3

## A Dream of Fear and Love

I had a dream that I was with two other men. We were walking along a beach and we came upon an amusement park like Coney Island in Brooklyn, New York. At the entrance to the park was a tunnel, like a tunnel of love—only this was the tunnel of fear. One of the young men was particularly anxious to go through the tunnel. The other young man was very resistant to going through. For some reason, it was decided that the two of them would go through and I would walk around on the outside. When they came out on the other end, the hair of the fellow who had been reluctant to go through had turned white. He fell on the ground in a fit, foaming at the mouth.

After the young man recovered, my companions proceeded farther into the park, but I decided to stay behind. I climbed into the top of the tunnel through an attic or loft-like door, much like the one on our barn when I was a boy. It was my intention to expose the inside of this place to show that it was just machinery that had caused my friend to become so fearful.

When I entered the loft, I found that indeed the place was filled with demonic creatures, just as one would see in a book on demonology. I looked at them and proceeded to walk into the room. As I did, they backed away respectfully. I realized that as long as I was unafraid of them they were powerless over me. For some reason, I was not afraid and as I stepped forward they kept moving back. Finally, I stopped and one of the more human-looking ones approached me and asked me if I would like to meet the devil himself. I said I would, and was led into a side room.

The devil was a little boy sitting in an aluminum lawn chair, with his arms resting regally on the arms of the chair and his head bent down to his chest as though he was pouting about something. I walked over to him, knelt down beside him, put my arms around him and said, "I love you. I love you." As I said that he began to shake and he started to scream, "No. No. You can't say that!" And puff! He disappeared. At that instant, I awoke.

*Fear is not of the present, but only of the past and future,*
*which do not exist.*
*There is no fear in the present when each instant*
*stands clear and separated from the past,*
*without its shadow reaching out into the future.*

T-15.I.8:2

The ego teaches that hell is in the future (T-15.I.4:3). "What if I get sick; what if I don't have enough money; what if there is nobody to take care of me; what if I die; what if all these terrible things happen?" These things are not happening *now*. Sin calls for punishment and this is frightening. Error calls for correction. Punishment is not correction. Fear arises when I think that I must expiate or pay for my sins by being punished, perhaps by "paying my debt to society." The Course is trying to help us awaken to the truth of our reality as Children of God. No one is punished for sins because the Sons of God are not sinners (T-6.I.16:5).

*How instantly the memory of God arises in the mind*
*that has no fear to keep the memory away!*

T-28.I.13:1

One of the most difficult ideas in the Course is the first sentence in the first paragraph of the first chapter: Principle Number One of the Fifty Miracles Principles. "There is no order of difficulty in Miracles. One is not 'harder' or 'bigger' than another. They are all the same. All expressions of love are maximal" (T-1.I.1). There is no unforgivable sin. Thinking there is makes sin real. Jesus goes to the cross to show us that even the most outrageous assault by one body onto another does not matter. Jesus was betrayed, abandoned, beaten, torn, and killed because of the projection of others onto him, but he did not see it as an attack (T-6.I.9:1–3). He knew that what was coming his way was coming out of ignorance and there is no need to attack ignorance.

This does not mean that our brother should be permitted to do hurtful things. Those who break society's laws go to jail because we don't know what else to do to stop them. Throughout the 1980s, I taught college classes inside Sing Sing Prison and Bedford Prison for Women, in New York State. There is a sign outside the gate at Sing Sing which says, "Sing Sing, New York State Correctional Institution." Although also deemed a place of correction, Sing Sing is a place for punishment. Little in the way of "correction" occurs inside Sing Sing. If we can't correct ourselves, is it likely that we can correct others? As long as we live in time, there will be another moment, another decision, and another opportunity to find out how completely we are willing to let go of sin, guilt, and fear. It all comes down to forgiving myself. I'm the only one who can change my mind.

## Forgiving the Self We Think We Made

If there is no ego system to hold on to, then neither is there need for any guilty past or future dread. There is nothing to be expiated for (T.13. II.9:2). We do not find freedom from guilt by making sin real, and then atoning for it. We do not experience freedom from guilt by beating up on ourselves. King David of the Bible, overwhelmed with guilt, literally covered himself in sackcloth and sat in the temple in ashes. Only by leaving the past in the past do I find freedom. We cannot obtain freedom from guilt by engaging in ritualistic practices. We are called upon to see things the way God does and that can only be done in the present.

## Finding Our Way Home

### 1. Look at It!

Lesson 39 from the Course, "My holiness is my salvation," asks us to search out our unloving thoughts, to take a good look at everything that stands between us and our salvation. We disengage ourselves from guilt by recognizing that what we are experiencing in the world is a reflection of what is inside. Look at judgment. See it without getting into it. I look at my special relationships—and see how I have projected my own fears into whatever it is I see. Guilt exists *only* in my mind. Fear exists *only* in my mind. As I have chosen to see the guilt and fear—so then it is that I can turn them over and let them go. This turnaround occurs, as I look at everything and realize I have made something out of nothing.

### 2. Ask for Help!

We cannot do it on our own. We do not need to do it on our own. Ask the Holy Spirit for help. By myself, I can do nothing. Living the Course, asking becomes a habit.

*Never attempt to overlook your guilt*
*before you ask the Holy Spirit's help. That is His function.*
*Your part is only to offer Him a little*
*willingness to let Him remove all fear and hatred,*
*and to be forgiven.*

T-18.V.2:3–5

Guilt is not fun. It does not "feel" good. If I'm feeling guilty, I can be sure this thought is coming from ego and not the Holy Spirit. If in doubt, choose again. As guilt is a projection within my own mind; it is also something I can change. Ideas leave not their source, therefore, the only place guilt can exist is in my mind. This thought is not in someone else's mind. Only I can change it. No matter how much I would like to rationalize it, guilt comes from my projections onto the world, which ultimately means onto myself.

> See no one, then, as guilty,
> and you will affirm the truth of guiltlessness unto yourself.
> In every condemnation that you offer the Son of God
> lies the conviction of your own guilt.

> T-13.IX.6:1–2

### 3.  Stop the Insanity

One friend describes how she knows when she's letting her mind be drawn toward some temptation to misperceive; she actually sees a stop sign in her mind. Who is in charge of the mind? It is possible to stop the ego mind's scheming, maneuverings, and misperceptions. It is possible to stop the process of constant analysis, interpretation, and projection. It is possible to stop the wandering off into guilt. If, however, we don't realize that we can stop insanity, we'll go on doing the same thing.

### 4.  Replace it!

"I do not like the way this makes me feel." It is often better to be wrong than right. It is better to be mistaken than to find justification for projection. It is wrong to be right when rightness is righteous indignation. No matter how attracted I am to them, no matter how justified I feel my attack thoughts might be; I can give them up. I can always choose once again. Heaven is a memory. The Holy Instant is a taste of eternity. Accepting Atonement means seeing no guilt in the past of anyone.

*For the Son of God is guiltless now,*
*and the brightness of his purity*
*shines untouched forever in God's Mind*

T-13.I.5:6

## Two Directions for Projection

There are two forms of projection. The first and most obvious is the condemnation I offer the world. The second is the projection I place upon myself. Having removed my projection onto the outside world, I may now turn my projection inward and make myself feel guilty for either what I think I have done, or failed to do in the past. This can be quite painful and often is. Projection is projection whether it is directed outward or inward. Either way, I am affirming the "seeming" reality of the ego. I cannot then acknowledge the Love of God. In order to be free of guilt, there must be *no* judgment either of another or myself. If there is no judgment—guilt is gone.

*Whenever the pain of guilt seems to attract you,*
*remember that if you yield to it,*
*you are deciding against your happiness,*
*and will not learn how to be happy.*

T-14.III.3:3

## You Are Not Guilty

I once went to see Dr. Helen Schucman, struggling with guilt over breaking off a relationship, which had caused the woman in question a great deal of pain. After I broke up with her, she became very upset and started acting out, calling at two and three in the morning just to awaken and annoy me. When the security guard at General Theological Seminary, where I was living, told her I was not in, she threw a cup of coffee in his face. She even physically attacked another woman I was dating at the time. I felt very guilty. Toward the end of my session with her, Helen reached out, lightly touched my knee, and said, "You know you're not guilty." I told Helen that I was sorry, but she was wrong. She did not understand. I was guilty. Yet on a deeper level, I understood what she meant. In the truth of who we are as Sons and Daughters of God, we cannot be guilty. I made a mistake. I acted in ignorance. I had to forgive myself and get on with life. This story has a wonderful ending as it never really ended. One night I forgot to take the phone off the hook. The woman in question started calling about two a.m. I got up and answered the phone. We talked until dawn and we worked it out. This "incident" occurred more than thirty-five years ago and she called the other day to wish me a happy birthday.

Lesson Number 46 from the Workbook, "God is the Love in which I forgive," provides the following direction. Say to yourself:

> *I cannot be guilty because I am a Son of God*
> *I have already been forgiven.*
> *No fear is possible in a mind beloved of God.*
> *There is no need to attack because love has forgiven me.*

W-46.6:3–6

## Giving Love Away

> *We have said that without projection there can be no anger,*
> *but it is also true that without extension there can be no love.*

T-7.VIII.1:1

A pathway out of hell comes in refocusing my mind away from the self to the whole, and thus, to my brother. My brother is the person I'm dealing with right now in the world—my daughter, my employer, the waitress who is serving breakfast. The main thing I can do for them is to let them be and/or to help them be who they are in truth by being Love. Thus, Lesson 36 says, "My holiness envelops everything I see." So it is that as I give, I receive; as I exempt my brother from the projection of guilt, so am I free of guilt myself. This is something I know the Holy Spirit would have me do. Doing God's will feels good naturally, just as being responsible about my bills or my health feels good naturally. It's proof of the fact that I am on the right track. Loving (helping) my brother in any way, the memory of love is returned to my mind. Being truly helpful is a road out of hell.

*From sin comes guilt as surely as forgiveness takes all guilt away.*

C-4.5:6

The central teaching of the Course appears five times in the Course in one simple phrase: "God's Son is guiltless." We are awakening to the memory of our Truth in God. The thoughts of sin, death, and hell contain no reality. Only what is eternal is real and God's Son *is* eternal. Eternal guiltlessness exists within the Mind of God. It cannot be otherwise. Enlightenment is an awakening to the truth that our Being is free from sin, guilt, and fear. Listening to the Holy Spirit is the choice for guiltlessness, happiness, and freedom. We are as we always have been. Our purity shines forever in the Mind of God. Everything else is a dream.

*Being responsible I see*
*My past was the only one that could be.*
*I could not have done it differently.*

*And so from guilt, I am set free.*
*No nostalgia, no remorse.*
*There really was no other course.*

—

*Where there is no guilt*
*there is a present—clearly seen*
*beautiful, free and wholly clean.*

# PART II

# The Metaphysics of Miracles

# CHAPTER 8

# The Dreaming of the World

## The Metaphysics of Miracles

*What if you recognized this world is an hallucination?*
*What if you really understood you made it up?*

T-20.VIII.7:3–4

We can't go far in our understanding of the Course without looking at the metaphysics behind the Course. Just as it was not
until Freud that we had a clear understanding of the basic dynamic of
the ego, it was not until Dr. Albert Einstein and the birth of the theory
of relativity that we had some idea about the illusory nature of space/
time. Metaphysics means that which is beyond physics. Meta means
after, beyond, or transcending, such as *meta*morphosis, as in the change
of a caterpillar into a butterfly. The butterfly comes after or goes beyond
the caterpillar. Physics examines the physical world. Metaphysics
comes after physics and examines the relationship between mind and
matter. An in-depth study of physics often leads to metaphysics and an
in-depth study of metaphysics can lead us to mysticism, and as it did for
Einstein—to God.

There is a section in Lewis Carroll's book, *Through the Looking-Glass,*
where Tweedledee comments to Alice that the Red King is dreaming
about her; and, were he to awaken, Alice would be *Nowhere* because she

is only something in his dream. Tweedledee says that Alice would go out like a candle if the King were to awaken. When Alice complains that their loud talking may wake the King, Tweedledum counters, "Well, it's no use you're talking about waking him when you are only one of the things in his dream. You know very well you're not real." Her frustration mounting, Alice insists, "I am real!" and begins to cry.

All of our time (waking and sleeping) is spent dreaming. The first words that we have recorded that Jesus said by way of ministry was, "Repent, for the Kingdom of Heaven is at hand" (Matthew 3:2). We might read that as "Wake up, for the Kingdom of Heaven is immediately available." "At hand" is not something which is going to come someday. It is something which is already here. It is simply a matter of our coming to the awareness of the presence of Heaven. Although the Course does not draw the following distinctions, we might talk of four different types of dreaming.

1. **The Hero of the Dream is** the body as we think of it as who we are in the dream.

2. **Our Secret Dream is** the mind's dream of sin, guilt, and fear. It's the story we tell ourselves all day long about ourselves.

3. **The Public Dream is** what we write on our resumes; what we tell the world about ourselves—what we think the world believes.

4. **The World's Dream** is what my friend, Jean Weston, calls "The Collusion of Illusion." This is the collective ego or the collective dream we share. It is the "appearance of reality," what is happening in the world of space and time—the world as it is objectified and solidified by the world itself. It is the world presented to us on television and in our history books.

*Your dreams contain many of the ego's symbols*
*and they have confused you.*

T-6.IV.6:5

## Watching Our Dreams

Freud called our nighttime dreams "the royal road to the unconscious." Our dreams represent our projections, fantasies, and fears. Paying attention to my dreaming, I begin to be aware of what is going on in a deeper dimension of consciousness. A study of dreams enables my understanding of the unconscious mind. There is usually some problem which is trying to be worked out within the dream. Likewise, in even the simplest of children's fairy tales, there is some problem which must be solved. We find ourselves within the dream on a journey, an expedition of sorts. We're trying to get home and the car won't start; we missed the bus; we're walking down the street; we don't have any shoes on and it is starting to snow. When we awake, we have a new set of problems. I must get up and get to work. I must deal with my kids, my health, and my angry boss. To escape it all, I come home at night and "veg out" in front of the television with a beer in hand, and thus, continue the dreaming of the world.

*We are such stuff as dreams are made of,*
*and our little life is rounded with a sleep.*

WILLIAM SHAKESPEARE, IN *THE TEMPEST*

Awakening in the morning, the dream is gone. The dreamer, however, is not gone and so the dream continues on. By night, I have wings and I can fly. Wakening, I can only fly inside machines. All the fantasies of the world are forms of daydreaming; misrepresentations and distortions in which we attempt to appropriate reality—to twist it into something it is not.

> *There is no world!*
> *This is the central thought the course attempts to teach.*
>
> W-132.I.6:2–3

Imagine what it would be like if you were not here—literally. If I have died and left this body; if my body has been cremated and there is absolutely nothing left of the body, would this whole life not seem like a dream which happened once upon a time in a land far, far away? Does your childhood not seem like a dream? Would this not be even more so if we literally were not here in this world—in this space and time?

> *All "things" and all sentiments are interpretations*
> *only, and interpretations cannot be real in any sense.*
>
> ENGLISH TAOIST, WEI WU WEI (1895–1986)

## Domestication and the Collusion of Illusion

The Australian Aborigines, perhaps the materially poorest people on earth—and the only group of people on earth who have no suicides in their culture—have always thought of this world as a dream. The native tribes in Venezuela also speak of *waking* life as a dream. The dreaming of the world includes all of society's rules, mores, morals, customs, beliefs, values, religions, myths, philosophies, psychological problems, and more. Our myths and religions run our lives. According to Scottish satirist Thomas Carlyle (1795–1881), "Popular opinion is the greatest lie in the world." Our families, social institutions, and the omnipresent media create, describe, and maintain "society's dream," and the collusion of illusion we all share. We are domesticated and addicted to dreaming as a dog is domesticated through a system of rewards and punishment.

*In solitude we have our dreams to ourselves,*
*and in company we agree to dream in concert.*

ENGLISH AUTHOR, DR. SAMUEL JOHNSON (1709–1784), IN *THE IDLER*

If a woman walks bare-breasted down almost any street in the United States, she can be arrested for indecent exposure. In certain South Pacific and African cultures, women walk around bare-breasted, and no one notices because it's not regarded as unusual. In some cultures, a woman must have not only her breasts covered but also her ankles, hands, face— everything. Each social code represents a diverse interpretation of reality. It is not that one is right and another is wrong. They are just different interpretations.

*Every child is born a mystic, then we draw him*
*toward the school and the education*
*and the serpent. The serpent is the civilization,*
*the culture, the conditioning.*

INDIAN SPIRITUAL TEACHER, OSHO (1931–1990)

From infancy onward, we are told what the world is. This teaching is incessant until we perceive the world correctly, that is, according to the prescribed formula of the culture in which we live. Eventually, we do not have to be domesticated. We want to please others, and act appropriately so we punish ourselves if we get out of line. Conform to the proper description of the world, make appropriate interpretations, and we are rewarded with money and prestige, fame and fortune, degrees and titles. The reality of day-to-day life consists of an unending stream of rarely questioned interpretations we share with the world.

## Trapped in the Dream

There is a scene in the movie *Saturday Night Fever* where John Travolta's brother comes home to tell his parents he has given up the priesthood. In explaining himself to Travolta's character, he says of their parents, "All I ever believed in was their image of me as a priest." We cannot awaken from a dream we think the world is dreaming for us. We only awaken when we become aware of the dreamer within the dream. Looking at a wall full of magazines in a bookstore, you can see *Gun World, Motor Home World, Antique World, Fishing World, Wrestling World,* and *Craft World,* to name a few. Pick a world. The world is just a view—it's just an attitude. There are lots of worlds in which we may invest. One evening, I asked my then-teenage daughter, Sarah, what she was watching on TV. She said it was a show called *The Real World.* "And what," I said, "is *The Real World*?" She said it was about teenagers who get drunk and have sex.

We live in the In-formation Age—an age coming into form. It is an age of cell phones, texting, social networking, e-mails, computers, and televisions all telling us what the world is. The more information I have, the more reinforcement I have about the constituents of reality. An electronic screen on the wall in our home tells us what is valuable and real; what's elegant, splendid, and sublime; what's offensive and repugnant, what's hip, what's hot, what's cool, and what's not. Daytime television is dominated by soap operas. In a soap opera, sin, guilt, fear, and hatred abound. One rule prevails: nobody gets to be happy! Here is the best of what the world has to offer: the finest homes, cars, furs, and jewels. Here too isolation, sorrow, suffering, and spiritual malnutrition proliferate. Watch a soap for only one minute. The characters are manipulative; everyone is out for themselves; they lie and cheat; no one is genuinely altruistic; no one is happy. So it is in the ego's world and so it is that we create our own soap operas and act them out with our families and friends, neighbors and co-workers.

## Just for Fun—Silly Ways We Make Up the World

As a part of our dreaming of the world, we sometimes do things and then forget why we started doing them. There are many funny illustrations of how this is done. Here is just one. I had a cocker spaniel named Joyful and, at the time, a home with a spacious dog-run out back— perfect for puppies. I had my Joyful dog bred and when the puppies were born, they all came out with tails. The father and mother did not have tails but the puppies all had tails. I didn't have the heart to cut them off. Consequently, my cocker spaniels grew up with tails. When they were about three or four months old and it was time to sell them and earn me some money, I was told by the breeder who was going to sell them for me that, "They have no value—they have tails." The best I could do was to give them away.

I decided this was silly, so I did some research to find out why it is necessary to cut off the tails of cocker spaniel puppies. A couple of hundred years ago, most of the world was rural. Cocker spaniels were then being raised in dirty barnyards so mud from the barnyard, cockleburs from the field—their own dung—everything got hung up in their long, hairy tails. The farmers, not wishing to have a ball of mud dragged into the house behind their dogs, started chopping off the tails of puppies to prevent this problem. Cocker spaniels now live in suburban homes and apartments. They never get close to muddy barnyards and cockleburs. And yet, if you don't cut that tail off . . .

After telling the cocker spaniel pups story in a public lecture, I once said, "Why are men circumcised?" and a woman in the group said, "Because they drag it in the mud." On another occasion, someone said, "Because, if you don't, they don't have any value. The best you can do is to try to give them away." And on still a third occasion, someone said, "Because women are always looking for 20 percent off." Male baby boys are taken within hours of birth into a nursery. They are strapped down with Velcro strips, and a portion of the most sensitive part of the human male anatomy is then cut off. Eighty percent of all adult American males are circumcised. The operation is often done procedurally without serious consultation with parents. Baby boys scream their heads off during this whole procedure. Here is "proof" of the fact that one is a body and a victim.

After services one Sunday, a woman asked if I would please pray for her little baby boy who was going into the hospital to have an operation. "My goodness," I said, "What's wrong?" "Well," she said, "You know the circumcision? They messed it up. We have to have reconstructive surgery done." "Why," I asked, "did you have him circumcised?" She said, "Well, my husband said, 'what happens when he is eleven years old, changing clothes in a gym someplace, and the other boys notice that he looks different? Let's fix it so he will not look different.'" It wasn't being done for religious or hygienic reasons; it was being done in conformity to tradition. I read the sermon of a nineteenth-century clergyman who described Heaven as a place where there were fine horses and carriages. His Heaven was an idealized representation of the world, perceived through nineteenth-century eyes.

*Every generation laughs at the old fashions,*
*but follows religiously the new.*

AMERICAN TRANSCENDENTALIST, HENRY DAVID THOREAU (1817–1862)

Saying there is no world, does not mean I deny the "seeming reality" of the world. To say there is no world, doesn't mean I'm not to be appreciative of beautiful mountains, rivers, and forests, flowers, animals, and good food. To say there is no world does not mean that I can do whatever I want without consequence. While in Rome, I do what normal Romans do—pay my taxes and observe the speed limit. I see the system for what it is without making it a problem. A Teacher of God is a "lover" of what presents itself: nature, music, or another soul. If I hate the world or my body, I make them real. After a lifetime of trying, tyrants must come with sadness to the realization that there is no world to possess and the dream of dominance was but a fleeting fantasy.

> *But healing is the gift of those who are prepared to*
> *learn there is no world, and can accept the lesson now.*
> *Some see it suddenly on point of death, and rise to teach it.*
> *Others find it in experience that is not of this world,*
> *which shows them that the world does not exist*
> *because what they behold must be the truth,*
> *and yet it clearly contradicts the world.*
>
> W-132.7:1, 3 & 4

## Become Lucid Dreamers

Knowing that I am "the dreamer of the dream," I can decide how I want to view the dream and I can continue to live in the world without taking things too seriously. Spirit is eternal; the activity of the ego is limited and destined to end in time. We make up the world and the world we make up is as a fantasy—sometimes a nightmare, sometimes very ordinary; sometimes quite beautiful.

> *You see the world that you have made,*
> *but you do not see yourself as*
> *the image maker. You cannot be saved from the world,*
> *but you can escape from its cause. This is what salvation means,*
> *for where is the world you see when its cause is gone?*
>
> W-23.4:1–3

Awareness of dreaming is the real work of God's teachers. Once I know I'm dreaming, I can change my perception of the dream. "I can see peace instead of this." Whatever "this" is, I can turn it over to the Holy Spirit. Happy dreams are still dreams. Now, however we see that we're in a classroom, not a prison. Now I dream of others' kindness and not their hurts; I dream of Heaven—no longer hell.

# CHAPTER 9

# I Am Not a Body

## DEATH AND THE EGO BODY IDENTITY

*The body is the central figure in the dreaming of the world.*
*There is no dream without it, nor does it exist*
*without the dream in which it acts as if it were*
*a person to be seen and be believed.*

T-27.VIII.1:1–2

The one phrase which is repeated more often than any other in the
Course is, "I am not a body. I am free." Ever feel as though you would
like to transcend the body—to get beyond the skin, to be free of its aches
and pains, the appetites and incessant needs of the body? Did you ever
wish that you did not have to wake this "thing" up in the morning? Who
is the "I" that awakens the body in the morning? Primitive man looking
at his face in a lake must have wondered about this "thing" looking back
at him. Plato called the body a tomb. Seneca said it was an inn, and Saint
Francis of Assisi lovingly called it "Brother Ass."

*The ego's fundamental wish is to replace God.*
*In fact, the ego is the physical embodiment of that wish.*
*For it is that wish that seems to surround the mind with a body,*
*keeping it separate and alone,*

*and unable to reach other minds except*
*through the body that was made to imprison it.*

W-72.2:1-3

## The Ego Body Identity

I know of no document as clear as the Course in its teaching about the body; and its clarification that we are not bodies. The body is a tiny fence around a grand and glorious idea. It is "a thought of separation" projected by the mind into form. Bodies are the very essence of the experience of separation and proof of physicality. The body is a very little segment of Heaven splintered off from the whole (T-18.VIII.2:5–6). They are obviously destructible and temporarily delimited in space and time. We are not our bodies and yet we are almost 100-percent identified with the body. According to the Course, the only thing we have not done completely is that we have not utterly forgotten the body. There may be moments when it fades from our sight but it never completely disappears (T-18.VII.2:1–2). There is plenty of evidence that we are bodies—look around. What do we see but other bodies? Vast sums of money are spent on cosmetics, clothes, and adornments for the body. The first thing each morning, we look in a mirror and affirm, for good or ill, the seeming reality of the body. How much time is given to appetites, compulsions, and hungers of the body we seem unable to control?

The body is a kind of escape vehicle for running away from God, giving us it seems, temporary autonomy from God. Seeing myself as a body makes the world real. Being preoccupied with the body and the dreaming of the world, it is easy to forget God. Anything a body does must first be a thought, whether that thought comes from mindfulness (sanity) or mindlessness (insanity). Good and bad, pain and pleasure appear as the mind judges the functions of the body. Pain and pleasure make the body real.

They are proof of the body's veracity, and therefore, the ego's existence. Pleasures, both physical and psychological, can make the world desirable and real. In pain, I hate the world and the body.

> *Out, out, brief candle!*
> *Life's but a walking shadow, a poor player,*
> *That struts and frets his hour upon the stage,*
> *And then is heard no more. It is a tale*
> *Told by an idiot, full of sound and fury,*
> *Signifying nothing.*

WILLIAM SHAKESPEARE'S *MACBETH* ACT 5, SCENE 5, 26–28

I asked a friend how he was doing and he said, "Well, at least I'm not six feet under." Whatever is "six feet under" has nothing to do with who we are. The ego has a need/hate relationship with the body, being seemingly inextricably connected with the body. While we may well "intuit" the illusory nature of the body, we simultaneously experience overwhelming evidence that we are bodies doomed to suffer, grow old and die, and then, amen.

> *The body is the ego's idol; the belief in sin made flesh and then*
> *projected outward. This produces what seems*
> *to be a wall of flesh around the mind, keeping it prisoner*
> *in a tiny spot of space and time.*

T-20.V.11:1–2

Pleasure involves an "activity" of the body, as does pain. How easily am I distracted by the murmurs, rumbles, and cravings of the stomach, the aches and pains of the body? How much time and money is spent in dealing with issues related to feeding, bathing, and pampering the body? Mouths are strange things, so are teeth, and the whole digestive and elimination system. Eating is an aggressive act. Animal bodies must die so that my body may live. Sex, too, is a strange activity if you think about it; but, let's not go there. One could easily do a comedy routine around the inelegant and awkward-looking nature of eating or sexuality. No doubt it has been done.

> *Appetites are "getting" mechanisms,*
> *representing the ego's need to confirm itself.*
> *This is as true of body appetites as it is of the so-called*
> *"higher ego needs." Body appetites are not physical in origin.*
>
> T-4.II.7:5–7

## Separation and the Body

We have admittedly ambivalent relationships with our bodies, sometimes loving them, sometimes hating them. We are critical of our own and others' bodies. If we are sick, overweight, or believe we are ugly, we may hate the body and feel that it is not good enough to be our home. Or, we may be proud of our bodies and hope or pretend that they will last forever. As they seemed to have a mind of their own and thinking they were evil, some of the early mystics sought to punish the body through mortification of the flesh, sitting outdoors in inclement weather, flagellating themselves with whips, and fasting to the point of death. All of this made the body more real than ever. Another group, the Libertines, saying that the body was not real, and therefore, inconsequential, thought they could do anything they wanted, and thus, engaged in a variety of excesses leading to bodily addictions and bodily ills.

The ego, seeking to keep the body from being found illusory, tries to project eternity into the body. The Pharaohs of Ancient Egypt were obsessed with trying to solidify monolithic images of themselves in stone, often scratching out the images of the Pharaohs who had gone before them. We raise children, write books, paint pictures, erect buildings, take pictures, have streets named after us and mausoleums constructed for the body, all in the grave hope of some earthly immortality.

> *No one believes there really was a time when he knew nothing of*
> *a body, and could never have conceived this world as real.*

> T-27.VIII.5:5

You may know that Presidents Thomas Jefferson and John Adams died the same day, July 4, 1826, exactly fifty years after the signing of the Declaration of Independence. They had been friends, but a rift developed between them. Toward the end of their lives, they renewed their friendship. In the last letter Jefferson sent to John Adams, he inquired about his health. John Adams wrote back saying that while he was fine, the house in which he lived had become quite dilapidated. The shingles had almost all fallen off (his hair was almost all gone). The windows were fogged over (he could no longer see). He was fine, but his body, like a decrepit old house, was just about to tumble over.

In the PBS series, "The Power of Myth," American journalist Bill Moyers (1934–present) asked the then-eighty-year-old mythologist Dr. Joseph Campbell (1904–1987), "What is it like being an octogenarian?" He said it was like driving an old car. It did not start as well in the mornings as it used to. It "chugged" up hills. It was covered with scars and wrinkles, and the tailpipe was starting to drag. He said he thought he was about ready to turn it in for a new model. Cars are the most "recycled" of all objects. Like our bodies, our cars are vehicles in which we move around. They give us status or the lack there of. As we animate or run our cars, so do we animate the body. The car has no life in it. It is just a "thing," as are our bodies. Eventually, just like the metal in my car, the carbon atoms which make up this body will decompose and reposition themselves in other forms of organic matter.

> *A major source of the ego's off-balanced state is its lack of discrimination between the body and the Thoughts of God.*
>
> T-4.V.2:1

> *If the mind can heal the body, but the body cannot heal the mind, then the mind must be stronger than the body.*
>
> T-6.V.A.2:6

The body cannot make the mind do anything but the mind can and does make the body do all sorts of things and the displacement of guilt onto the body makes the body sick. The body is, itself, neutral and an instrument of the mind. On its own, it cannot be guilty. So, the question is then, what does the mind do with the body?

## Watching the Body

Watch the body dispassionately. Notice the ego-body distractions as it speaks to us of its appetites and needs. "I'm hungry." "I need to pee." "I need to sleep." A friend says, "I can't get going until I have my cup of coffee in the morning." Who is the "I" that can't get going without the coffee? Who runs this machine? Who thrusts the hand inside a bag of potato chips? Is the ego running the show or is there a higher perspective?

> *First drink, man drinks wine.*
> *Second drink, wine drinks wine.*
> *Third drink, wine drinks man.*
>
> JAPANESE PROVERB

Watch the body and see what seems to be upsetting about it. Do I "need" the drink? Maybe "I" don't need it. If the body is preoccupied with pain, it captures my attention and holds it outside of the mind. From a place of Vision or right-mindedness we see—even though the body may be in pain, there is a part of our mind that can step back, transcend the body, watch what is happening, and choose peace.

*You see the flesh or recognize the spirit.*

T-31.VI.1:1

How easily do I dissociate, go unconscious, or get caught up in some bodily-based addiction? Do I even "try" to control bodily impulses? When an appetite arises rather than "going for it," can I just wait? Do I really need to go there? Appetites diminish when not fed. Food, especially too much of it, begins, after a period of fasting, to look heavy and repulsive. It is helpful to have a certain objectivity when it comes to the body; not to its neglect but simply a dropping off of its incessant importance. Disconnecting from obsessiveness of the body also facilitates reuniting with the mind which is, after all, the thing which really runs the show. Not being so obsessed, I can then, with greater clarity, choose for the inner voice of reason rather than the outer voice of insanity. I can choose not to let the ego-body run the show.

*The Holy Spirit's messengers are sent far beyond the body,*
*calling the mind to join in holy communion and be at peace.*

. . . .

*Pain is the only "sacrifice" the Holy Spirit asks,*
*and this He "would" remove.*

T-19.IV.B.3:1&7

A friend says that I should stop telling people they are not bodies and I say, "If I seem to be over-emphasizing the fact that we're not bodies, it's because we have so over-stressed the seeming reality of the body that we need to go a bit the other way to get back into balance." The body is a learning device for the mind, a mechanism, a vehicle, a means of locomotion, and a computer. Placed in Spirit's hands, it can be a helpful tool on the journey Home. The best thing we can do with the body is to turn it over to Spirit.

> *Child of God, you were created to create the good, the*
> *beautiful and the holy. Do not forget this. The Love of God, for a*
> *little while, must still be expressed through one body to another,*
> *because vision is still so dim.*

T-1.VII.2:1–5

## A Harp for the Soul

The famous pianist Ignacy Jan Paderewski once appeared on stage with a violin. He told the audience that it was one of the most expensive violins in the world. He proceeded to play a stunning number. At its conclusion, the audience stood with uproarious applause. After the applause had died down, Paderewski motioned for the audience to sit down. He then took the violin and smashed it over his knee. As everyone gasped in horror, Paderewski said, "I was only kidding. It was a cheap imitation." Then he said, "I will now play a violin that really is one of the most expensive in the world." He then played a number, as magnificent as the first. Only a few said they could really hear the difference. We are not bodies. We're the ones who play the song. It's how the song is played that makes all the difference. Lebanese poet Kahlil Gibran (1883–1931) called the body a harp for the soul. Spirit makes the music of our lives. Under the guidance of the ego, the body communicates pain, fear, separation, despair, and anger. With Spirit's guidance, it can communicate healing, love, unity, and joy.

Beyond the appearance of the body—past the mascara, face-lifts, wigs, porcelain teeth, and elevator shoes—is something that radiates us, thinks us, and feels us. That something is the Spirit which gives life. The thing which will one day lie in the ground or be burnt into ashes has no meaning. Someday it will disappear. It seems like a necessity, and we do not know who we would be without it; and yet, beyond the body, beyond the stars, and everything we see, shines a radiant light of True Being (T-21.1:8:1).

## Looking at Death

A five-year-old girl, returning home from her great-grandmother's funeral in the back of a limousine with her other great-grandmother, asked, "Where did Grandma go?" "We believe she went to be with God," the other grandmother replied. "How old was she?" asked the little girl. "She was eighty years old." "How old are you?" "I'm eighty-three." And the little girl said, "I hope God hasn't forgotten you!"

*You can rest in peace only because you are awake.*

T-8.IX.4:9

Love does not have a form. Eternity does not have a form. God does not have a form. Truth does not have a form. Thought is life and thought does not have a form. Life is not dependent on form. To say that life is

eternal does not mean that we go from one body (form) to another—
that would be a continuation of dreaming. Why go from story to story
to story, from drama to drama to drama? Why not awaken from the
dream?

> *In the ultimate sense, reincarnation is impossible.*
> *There is no past or future, and the idea of birth into a body has no*
> *meaning either once or many times.*
> *Reincarnation cannot, then, be true in any real sense.*
>
> M-24.1:1–3

Anything that rusts, rots, decays, or turns from one form back into
another, is not permanent, and, therefore, not eternal. Only Spirit is eternal. Jesus did not resist the crucifixion because he knew he was not a
body; and, he went to the cross to show us that although his body could
be killed, He could not. As a line in Martin Luther's hymn "A Mighty
Fortress" says: "The body they may kill, God's Truth abideth still. His
Kingdom is forever." Light and darkness, knowledge and perception, life
and death are irreconcilable. All there is, is life. To lose a body is to lose a
body. Billions of people have already done it. Death is not the end. It's not
the beginning. It is nothing.

> *If the story of the wandering Jew be true,*
> *indeed if there was a man who could not die,*
> *would he not be the unhappiest of men?*
>
> DANISH THEOLOGIAN, SOREN KIERKEGAARD (1813–1855)

Nothing physical is immortal. By definition, that which exists in
time has form. God is formless. The ego is only understood by transcending it; at which point, we have no use for it. There is no eternity
in the body—the form of the thing is never the thing. The only thing

which can die (because it never was alive) is the ego. What gives life is not the body. What gives life is the Mind (Spirit). Bodies disappear into the nothingness from which they came, just like a dream disappears when we wake up in the morning. Illusions cannot be a part of eternity.

*For what is it to die, but to stand naked in the sun*
*and melt into the wind?*

LEBANESE POET, KAHLIL GIBRAN (1883–1931), IN *THE PROPHET*

An American tourist once paid a visit to renowned Polish rabbi Hofetz Chaim. He was astonished to see that the rabbi's home was merely a simple room, with only books, a table, a chair, a bed, a sink and a simple cabinet. The tourist asked, "Rabbi, where is your furniture?" Hofetz Chaim replied, "Where is yours?" The puzzled American asked, "Mine? But I'm only a visitor here. I'm only passing through." The rabbi replied, "So am I." Spirit is immortal, and immortality is an endless state. At death, form dissolves into formlessness. Only the illusory shell, the body, is lost. Without the body there are no accoutrements which go with the body. Without the body there is no space/time; there is no world.

One of the most central ideas in the Course is that we are not bodies. Bodies are obvious expressions of separation. We are Mind. Bodies cannot join—Minds can. Bodies are different. Minds are not different because there is only one Mind and we are one only at the level of Mind. A fellow minister told me that her mother's last words on the occasion of her death, at the age of 100 were, "Good morning."

*When your body and your ego and your dreams are gone,*
*you will know that you will last forever.*
*Perhaps you think this is accomplished through death,*
*but nothing is accomplished through death,*
*because death is nothing.*
*Everything is accomplished through life,*
*and life is of the mind and in the mind.*
*The body neither lives nor dies,*
*because it cannot contain you who are life.*

T-6.V.A.1:1–4

# CHAPTER 10

---

# Always Must Be Now

## THE PRACTICE OF PATIENCE

*Time is a trick, a sleight of hand, a vast illusion in which figures
come and go as if by magic. Yet there is a plan behind appearances
that does not change. The script is written.*

*When experience will come to end your doubting has been set.*

*For we but see the journey from the point at which it ended, looking
back on it, imagining we make it once again;*

*reviewing mentally, what has gone by.*

W-158.4:1–5


*God wills you perfect happiness now.
Is it possible that this is not also your will?*

T-9.VII.1:8


T hings seem to happen sequentially, in time, one after another. We
have past, present, and future. We make up seconds, minutes, hours,
weeks, and months and then forget that these "measuring devices" are all
of our own making. We could have made up months with three weeks

of ten days each. We could have seconds with different length than what we've constructed. Days could be made up with a different set of what we call hours. We make up measuring devices and then we live as though what we've made up is reality. Time makes sense when we perceive events moving in a linear sequence from the past, through the present, into the future. According to Moses Maimonides (1135–1204, Spain, Egypt), a foremost mystic in medieval Judaism, the idea of God creating the world at some point in time is itself a projection from time-bound circumstances. Time is the ego's way of keeping everything from happening at once.

*For us believing physicists, the distinction between past,*
*present, and future is only a stubbornly persistent illusion.*

GERMAN-BORN PHYSICIST, ALBERT EINSTEIN (1879–1955)

Einstein's secretary once asked him if he could explain to her the theory of relativity, and he said, "Two hours with a beautiful woman seems like two minutes. Two minutes on a hot stove seems like two hours. That is relativity!" Time can speed up. It can slow down. What if it stopped? Would that not give us a wholly new perspective? Scientists tell us that if we could travel at the speed of light—186,000 miles per second—time would stop! We live in time, in fact, we're innately caught in time.

*And Jesus said unto him, No man,*
*having put his hand to the plough*
*and looking back, is fit for the Kingdom of God.*

LUKE 9:62

*Be still today and listen to the truth. Be not deceived by voices of*
*the dead, which tell you they have found the source of life and offer*
*it to you for your belief. Attend them not, but listen to the truth.*

W-106.2:2–4

The voices of the dead are traditions; the ego frame of reference—the way we have always looked at the world. In order to see, we have to stop making up the world. We have to be still and listen. We are easily preoccupied with the past—lost loves, unfulfilled ambitions, incomplete degrees, feelings of nostalgia, regret, and remorse are all part of the dreaming mind. Where is a grievance? A grievance can exist only in my mind and it can only be about something in the past, even if it was only a moment ago. Dr. William Thetford was once asked how one can know if they are progressing in the Course and he said, "You can tell by how quickly you're willing to let a grievance go." Living the Course means not only more quickly letting go of grievances; it means we don't have grievances because we do not create them.

*Unless you learn that past pain is an illusion,*
*you are choosing a future of illusions and losing the many*
*opportunities you could find for release in the present.*

T-13.IV.6:5

I watched an old black-and-white movie in which a fellow falls in love with a girl. Then, something he thinks is unforgivable happens. He finds out something unpleasant about her past. He rejects her, runs away, gets into an accident, and develops amnesia. When she finds out about the accident, she rushes to find him but he does not remember her and low and behold, he falls in love with her all over again without the memory of any grievance.

A friend tells the story of being married to an alcoholic who abused her, not physically but psychologically. When he died, she said the anger she had toward him disappeared in an instant—like someone had opened a valve on a drain; the pain dissipated, and all that was left was the love she felt for him. Forgiveness, says the Course, is selective remembering based not on your selection (T-17.III.1:3). Holding a grievance is painful, whether it be a grievance we hold against others or ourselves. Only forgiving ourselves and letting it go brings peace.

> *You consider it "natural" to use your past experience*
> *as the reference point from which to judge the present.*
> *Yet this is "unnatural" because it is delusional.*
> *When you have learned to look on everyone*
> *with no reference at all to the past,*
> *either his or yours as you perceived it,*
> *you will be able to learn from what you see now.*
>
> T-13.VI.2:1–3

Without memory, there could be no guilt. Remorse, penitence, and painful memories arise only in association to past events. The older we get, the more past we have, the greater the pull to live in the past. The younger we are, the more we tend to "project" the future. Did you ever wake up in the morning and, before getting up, start a rehearsal of a variety of mistakes made in the past and "if only" you had chosen differently? We have guilt in the past. We say, "If only—if only. . . If only, I had made a series of different choices in the past, I would have a different present." That is true. *If* we had made a series of different choices in the past, we *would* have a different present; but, *we did not* make a series of different choices in the past, so we now have our present.

Only through forgiveness of ourselves for thinking we should have a different past can we undo the effects of the past (guilt) in the present. Forgiving ourselves comes in the acceptance of the fact that we could never have a different past. The more focused I am, the less distracting is any past. One of the things we can say for sure about the past is that it is not here now. Whatever happened in the past—whatever guilt or blame we place upon ourselves or others—does not exist in the moment unless I try to drag it into the moment.

*Perhaps you do not yet fully realize*
*just what holding grievances does to your mind.*
*It seems to split you off from your Source and make you unlike Him.*

W-68.1:5–6

I knew a man whose father was a rough, difficult man. The son had a lot of trouble dealing with his father and often felt he hated him. Then one day the father, who was now getting older, was hit by a car while crossing the street. A few days later, he suffered a stroke. He never quite recovered. After that his mind changed and he became more childlike—more loving. Now the man whom the son had hated was altogether different and dependent upon his son to care for him. What a dilemma! The old man, who the son had hated, was no longer hateful. Now, he was loving. As the son was willing to let go of the past, a healing occurred in him and in the relationship. All that was left, all that was real between them was love. It is always like that: buried within, sometimes not even too deeply, love is trying to find a way out past all the trappings of the ego.

*The holy instant is the Holy Spirit's most useful learning device for*
*teaching you love's meaning. For its purpose is to suspend judgment*
*entirely. Judgment always rests on the past, for past experience*
*is the basis on which you judge. Judgment becomes impossible*
*without the past, for without it you do not understand anything.*

T-15.V.1:1–4

*Take therefore no thought for the morrow:*
*for the morrow shall take thought for the things of itself.*

MATTHEW 6:34

## What If?: Fear and the Future

I turned on the television one evening and checked out some favorite channels. There is a show about the *Apocalypse*, one on *Life after People*, one called *Doomsday* and another on the ten most likely ways in which the world will end—not *if* but *when*. We have "if only" in the past, and "what if" in the future. "What if I get sick?" "What if I do not have enough money?" "What if there is nobody to take care of me?" The ego teaches that hell is in the future, when we get found out, when the body becomes diseased, when we die and must then relinquish our hold on the world. Time in the ego's system is a teaching device for compounding guilt. It is an opportunity for me to look at all the mistakes I've made. There is, however, no fear in the present. In this moment, and this moment alone, each Holy Instant stands clear and unblemished by shadows of the past. I cannot be present if I'm living in the past or projecting the future. The younger we are, the more we project the future. The older we are, the more we project the past and when we are middle-aged we are nowhere, living in both the past and the future, and then we have what we call a mid-life crisis.

*Patience is natural to the teacher of God.*
*All he sees is a certain outcome, at a time perhaps*
*unknown to him as yet, but not in doubt.*

M-4.VIII.1:2–3

## Patience

Stopping along a country road, a city-slicker noticed a farmer lifting one of his pigs up to an apple tree and holding the pig there as it ate one apple after another. The farmer repeated this with a second and then a third pig. "Maybe I don't know what I'm talking about," said the city-slicker, "but if you just shook the tree so the apples fell to the ground, wouldn't it save a lot of time?" "Time?" said the farmer, "What does time matter to a pig?"

Coming downstairs in our house in the morning, I sometimes see our cat, Pockets, sitting by the sliding glass door leading out onto the deck waiting to be let in. Sometimes, when I open the door, he just sits there. Pockets has all the time in the world. Animals do not "think" about time. They do not make an investment in time. They don't have time for it. Animals do not have clocks, and therefore, no seconds, minutes, or hours. Animals are more "immediate" than we are and their simple, uncomplicated presence is one of the reasons we love them so much.

## Timelessness Is Reality

The word *patience* comes from *patient,* meaning someone who endures an illness. Patience comes as we find freedom from time. The center of a cyclone is a point of absolute stillness. Around the outside there is an immense amount of chaos. In the center, everything stops, and there is complete silence. The Holy Spirit invites us to step into the center where chaos has stopped and only eternity remains. From this point, we may see chaos and yet not be part of it. The crucifixion could be seen as a moment of absolute chaos, yet Jesus does not see it this way, which is what makes him the Christ. *Eternity* is timelessness. God is timelessness. Love is timelessness. Christ is timelessness. In timelessness, things just are. Being is a state in which the mind is in communication with everything that is real (T-4.VII.4:4). There is nothing to control or manipulate. Jesus stepped away from eternity, came into time, but remembered eternity. We step away from eternity, and then we get caught in time; we get caught in the past and our histories; we get caught in dramas and lose sight of eternity.

*Arrogance is the denial of love,*
*because love shares and arrogance withholds.*
*As long as both appear to you to be desirable the concept of choice,*
*which is not of God, will remain with you.*
*While this is not true in eternity it "is" true in time,*
*so that while time lasts in your mind there will be choices.*
*Time itself is your choice.*
*If you would remember eternity,*
*you must look only on the eternal.*

*If you allow yourself to become preoccupied with the temporal,*
*you are living in time. As always,*
*your choice is determined by what you value.*
*Time and eternity cannot both be real,*
*because they contradict each other.*
*If you will accept only what is timeless as real,*
*you will begin to understand eternity and make it yours.*

T-10.V.14:1–9

Our basic problem is arrogance. What I see is a dream, created by me. In this dream, I make myself right. Making myself right is separation. It is not a choice that occurred in the past. It is a moment-by-moment decision. My desires to be special are my own present miscreations coming from the arrogant demand of my ego.

"God and the soul," says German Meister Eckhart (1260–1326), "are not in space-time. They belong to the realms that are intrinsically or essentially real." "Time ends," he says, "where there is no before or after." We perceive, says Eckhart, only a shadow of the real, living in a world created and sustained by our own cognition. Or as American psychic Edgar Cayce expressed it, "There is no time; it is one time. There is no space; it is one space." Space is as much an illusion as time, as space is the projection of separation. Without space there would be no separation.

*Do not dwell in the past; do not dream of the future,*
*concentrate the mind on the present moment.*

BUDDHA (563 BCE–483 BCE)

## Patience, Focus, and Flow

In the mystical experience, the mind is concentrated in the moment. People feel alive during emergencies because the moment calls for focus and full attention. What is happening is precisely what is going on in the moment. We've all had the experience of needing to study for an exam, or needing to concentrate on something at work and in that process, we discover that focusing the mind reduces time. The monkey-mind jumps from one distraction to another. By doing what we are called to do—in the moment—right now—we reduce time by not allowing for delay, or distraction. Studies on happiness show that people who are able to "focus" are happier people because of their ability to live in the moment. This heightened focus also enables them to get into a "flow," where it is easy to lose track of time.

Having made time, the ego easily becomes a slave to time. If there is no time, I can't be in a hurry. We have all the time in the world precisely because we are not of the world. We say of someone who does not complain, that that individual has the "patience of a saint." Why do we equate patience with saintliness unless we know that, in fact, patience is saintly? Teachers of God are patient. They can afford to be. If you truly knew that this moment is the only time there is, would you chose to argue with a brother?

*It is believed by most that time passes;*
*In actual fact, it stays where it is.*
*This idea of passing may be called time,*
*it is, however, an incorrect idea,*
*for since one sees it only as passing,*
*One cannot understand that it stays just where it is.*

JAPANESE ZEN MASTER, DOGEN ZENJI (1200–1253)

Time does not move; it stands still. For this reason, our relationship with God is vertical rather than horizontal. It is in precisely this moment that complete salvation is available for us. Truth is, there is no time and that is literally the end of the story.

*One source of perceived discouragement from which you may suffer*
*is your belief that this takes time, and that the results of the Holy*
*Spirit's teachings are far in the future. This is not so. For the Holy*
*Spirit uses time in His Own way, and is not bound by it.*

T-15.I.1:3

## Always Has No Direction

A minister is addressing his congregation and he says, "All those who want to go to Heaven, stand up." Everyone stood up except one older man who stubbornly kept his seat. The minister looked at him and said, "Don't you want to go to Heaven?" "No," said the man. So the minister said, "Do you mean to tell me you don't want to go to Heaven when you die?" The man responded, "Of course, I want to go to Heaven when I die. I thought you meant now." If you were offered the opportunity for enlightenment right now—would you take it? I occasionally ask this question in workshops and very few people raise their hands saying yes they would.

Not needing to live in time, not needing to live according to an image, or be caught in a drama enables our experience of eternity. It is possible to be so present that past (guilt) and future (fear) lose their significance and imprison us no longer. There is no sin, no guilt, and no fear in Heaven. Heaven is *here* because there is no other place, and Heaven is *now* because there is no other time (M-24.6:4–7). Heaven is immediately available, but the ego puts God off until tomorrow, until the very last moment; until time runs out.

> *Those who are certain of the outcome*
> *can afford to wait, and wait without anxiety.*
>
> M-VIII.1:1

I was talking with a friend and asked, "What have you been doing?" She said, "Nothing," and I asked if she had been doing nothing well. To stop thinking would be the end of the ego, so the ego must worry to stay alive. The ego must have problems. Otherwise, there is no ego. There are no problems in eternity. God does not have a problem; to the ego everything is problematic.

> *The memory of God comes to the quiet mind.*
>
> T-23.I.1:1

As I travel to give lectures, I usually stay in the homes of Course students. This includes the home of one 90-plus-year-old woman, a student/teacher named Mary Louise Hamilton. Last time I was with her, I asked her how she spent her time and she said, "I don't watch television much anymore except to check on the weather. I don't read very much anymore. I don't talk to too many people. I'm not lonely. I will admit to one addiction. I love doing crossword puzzles. Mostly," she said, "I sit and think about God." I knew that she meant what she said. The goal of the Course is peace and happiness. Can you imagine that there is anything you want more?

*When peace comes at last to those who wrestle*
*with temptation and fight against the giving in to sin;*
*when the light comes at last into the mind given to contemplation;*
*or when the goal is finally achieved by anyone, it always comes*
*with just one happy realization; "I need do nothing."*

T-18.VII.5:7

## Impatience

We live in a world where we wait in lines at the bank, the grocery store, the ATM, the movies, and so on. We wait in our cars for accidents, crowded conditions, and construction delays. Waiting in line is a good time to practice patience. It is a good time to meditate. The moment I notice I am being impatient, I can say, "I can be patient now!" This line isn't going to move for a while, so it's better to wait with peace of mind than a distressed mind. Waiting in line is simple. Just observe. Watch the world with a tranquil mind. If the cat doesn't go out the door when I open it, or my child takes a long time to get ready, I may put my foot behind my cat and give him a nudge or I may ask my child to hurry up. I can do it, however, without being upset and annoyed. I can do it with a tranquil mind. Remembering Home is being Home.

*Your patience with your brother is your patience with yourself.*
*Is not a child of God worth patience?*
*I have shown you infinite patience*
*because my will is that of our Father, from*
*Whom I learned of infinite patience.*
*His Voice was in me as It is in you,*
*speaking for patience towards the Sonship. . . .*

T-5.VI.11:4–7

We wander about doing all sorts of things other than God's Will; yet, God does not scold us, nor does He desert us. No matter how far we wander away; no matter how much we may block our ears, the Holy Spirit always gently calls us Home. God has infinite patience with us. Can we not demonstrate some patience with our brothers?

> *Only infinite patience produces immediate effects.*
> *This is the way in which time is exchanged for eternity.*
> *Infinite patience calls upon infinite love,*
> *and by producing results now it renders time unnecessary.*

T-5.VI.12:1–3

There is nothing to be in a hurry for. There is not someplace else to go. After all, no matter wherever we go—there we are. A woman came to me anxious to gain some spiritual perspective. A friend told her about the Course and she was upset when I said I had no copies of the Course to give her; but, a new shipment was coming in and I said, I would get a copy to her the next week. She came to the study group for four weeks and then quit. One day, I bumped into her in the grocery store and asked her if she was still studying the Course. "No," she said, "that is way too slow." She needed answers now. I told her the answer was available now, but she was looking for *magic* not a *miracle*; and, I had no magic to give her.

If we're going to learn a musical instrument, we need to practice, practice, practice. If we're going to learn a foreign language—we've got to "hang in there" in order to "get it." Mastery of the Course comes with patience. The complexities that bind us in knots took us a lifetime to develop; and letting go is often slow. Answers are available now but we have to be patient to experience the results. Wherever you are—be there!

**A Holy Instant is** as long as it takes to reestablish perfect sanity, perfect peace, and perfect love (T-15.I.4:1). It is as long as it takes to trade hell for Heaven. It is as long as it takes to remember immortality. The Holy Instant is a moment of aliveness, a time in which we give and receive perfect communication with all minds (T-15.IV.6:5). It is a moment in which we choose forgiveness over a grievance. My friend, Reverend Ellyn Kravette, tells the story of her relationship with her mother. They were stuck in power and control issues. Her mother was ninety-six when she died and Ellyn took care of her during the last ten years of her life. During that time, she moved to the in-between world and she forgot about her grievances. One day, she called Ellyn over to her bed and she said, "We have such a lovely relationship, how did that happen?" There is a place outside of time where a choice is made for forgiveness instead of guilt. It is this instant and every instant in which truth and love abide. It is a time in which we give and receive in perfect communication. It is a miniature of Heaven. It is eternity.

> *On this side of the bridge to timelessness you understand nothing.*
> *But as you step lightly across it, upheld by timelessness,*
> *you are directed straight to the Heart of God.*
> *At its center, and only there, you are safe forever,*
> *because you are complete forever.*

T-16.IV.13:6—8

The Course is not about the world.
It's not about the body.
It's not about time.
It's about the Mind.

*If we can get the mind to be still—we see.*
*We always have been. We always will be.*

# PART III

# LIVING *A COURSE IN MIRACLES*

## The Practical Application

# CHAPTER 11

# The Inner Teacher, the Ego, and God's Plan for Salvation

## THE ROLE OF THE HOLY SPIRIT IN *A COURSE IN MIRACLES*

*All miracles mean life, and God is the Giver of life.*
*His Voice will direct you very specifically.*
*You will be told all you need to know.*

PRINCIPLE NUMBER 4 OF THE FIFTY MIRACLES PRINCIPLES

OF *A COURSE IN MIRACLES* T-1.I.4

When something really good happens, we say, "Thank you, God!" When something really bad happens, we say, "Oh God, please no!" In such moments are we not at least hopeful that there is a God who hears us? Helen Schucman said that the purpose of the Course was to help us come to an awareness of the presence of the Inner Teacher. Becoming progressively aware of the Inner Teacher enables our finding a way home.

There is a Self, a loving, wise, gentle, guide who knows the way Home. This Self knows our deepest heart's desire and the decision we need to make at each and every instant. Being concerned or obsessed with the world—with our bodies and our relationships, it is easy to "fall" into ego and then get caught in confusion, bewilderment, perplexity, and depression. Inner life can be neglected, repressed, ignored, and, sometimes, but not ever entirely, forgotten.

*There is guidance for each of us,*
*And by lowly listening we shall hear the right words.*

AMERICAN POET, RALPH WALDO EMERSON (1803–1882)

Listening to the Holy Spirit instead of the ego is a matter of reawakening to the awareness that there is an Inner Guide. We don't have to depend upon ourselves alone. There is a line in an old, African American hymn made popular by Harry Belafonte in the 1960s titled, "There is No Hiding Place Down Here." There is no running away from God. We can try, but repressing awareness of the Holy Spirit means living in an artificial fantasy world and deep inside we know it. We can no more avoid God than He can avoid us. So we might as well say, "Hello God, I'm ready and willing to follow your lead. I will not run. I will not hide. I will not be afraid of your love."

*This is a course in how to know yourself.*
*You have taught what you are,*
*but have not let what you are teach you.*

T-16.III.4:1–2

The Holy Spirit is a formless unified thought, an indwelling spirit, a spark, a counselor, a comforter, a healer, and a mediator. That which is eternal has always been available. Things are only "new" when we come upon them for the first time. Socrates, Plato, and the Stoics of Ancient Greece spoke of this Inner Teacher as the "inner genius." Confucius called it the *Superior Man.* The Zoroastrians of ancient Persia called it the *Spenta Mainu.* In Judaism, it's called the *Ruach* (Breath) *Hakodesh*

(Holy) or *Shechina,* which embodies the nurturing aspects of God given to us at the moment of separation in order to help us find our way back to Home.

St. Paul, in Corinthians, refers to this teacher as indwelling Spirit. In Islam—Angels, *extensions of the thoughts of God,* are protective figures that "light" our way. It is the same Angel Gabriel who tells Mary of the coming of Jesus who dictates the Qur'an to Mohammed. Throughout the New Testament and the Course, the terms *Counselor, Comforter, Healer, Guide, Teacher,* and *Mediator* are used to describe different qualities of One Holy Spirit.

> *As the Father in his simple nature gives his Son birth naturally,*
> *so truly does he give him birth in the most inward part of the Spirit,*
> *and that is the inner world.*
>
> GERMAN MYSTIC, MEISTER ECKHART (1260–1326)

Meister Eckhart, spoke of "the little spark" that enlightens our way. On eight different occasions the Course also speaks of this little spark in the mind (T-11.in.3:6). New England transcendentalist Henry David Thoreau (1818–1862,) said that the degree to which we are true to ourselves is the degree to which we pay attention to inner intelligence. Throughout the history of mystical philosophy, this inner guide is referred to as our Self, Higher Self, True Self, Jesus, The Christ, The Holy Spirit, and The Voice for God. There is a *spark* within our mind, an extension of the light of God.

> *Turn toward the light, for the little spark in you is part of a light*
> *so great that it can sweep you out of all darkness forever.*
> *For your Father is your Creator, and you are like Him.*
>
> T-11.III.5:6

## The Comforter

African American Civil Rights leader Martin Luther King Jr. (1929–1968) told a story of once being terribly afraid. His life and those of his family had been threatened. One night when he could not sleep, he got up and went and sat in the dark at the kitchen table. He was thinking maybe he should call off a Civil Rights march. There in the middle of the night, in the dark, he began to pray. He asked, "What am I supposed to do?" This is a very good prayer. Like all prayer, it is asking but it also a way of saying, "Holy Spirit, help me. I want to see this the way you do." King then sat quietly and there in the middle of the night despite his terror, he said he heard a voice say, "Do not be afraid." He got up with a renewed sense of peace and went on with the march despite the threats that were converging upon him.

I've been offering workshops on listening to inner guidance for several years. At each workshop, I ask folks to tell me about experiences in which they have felt as though they received some form of inner guidance, not intuitively, but things they thought they had actually heard. I wrote down what I was told and after many years, I collected hundreds of things people told me they heard, usually just a sentence or two. Sometimes, it was the same thing heard by someone else in yet another time and place. We tend to remember best those things which happen in dramatic life-changing moments of crash and burn, when we really needed help. We hear when we give up trying to figure life out and in desperation cry out for help. What is heard at this point is something very comforting and reassuring. It is never anything that would upset or disturb. As the angels said to the shepherds on the hillside at the time of the birth of Jesus, "Fear not."

Here are some examples of what people said they heard:

- "Haven't I always taken care of you?"
- "I'm here to help you."

- "I've been waiting for you."
- "I have always loved you."
- "You are never alone."
- "You just need to be."
- "You need do nothing."
- "You are on the right track."
- "You are my beloved daughter in whom I am well-pleased."
- "You never did anything wrong."
- "There is another way to look at this."
- "This need not be."
- "Trust me!"
- "It takes time to be healed."
- "There will always be enough."
- "Everything is going to be okay."
- "Let me handle this."

A man who was walking out of the front door of an office building where he had just been fired, cried out, "Help!" and He heard, "You just got help."

These are "openings," "reassurances" which come during dramatic moments when there is need for comfort and support. This is not, however, the usual way in which the Holy Spirit speaks to us. When we really need help, *sometimes* the comforter comes during our "hour of greatest need." It is best, however, not to wait for crisis in order to be in communication. Nor do we hear an actual voice. The "teacher," "guide," "healer" comes to us gently during more peaceful moments when studying, meditating, in our dreams, in doing the Workbook Lessons of the Course, just relaxing, perhaps while going for a walk, or perhaps when we're lying awake in bed in the morning.

> *God whose love is everywhere*
> *can't come to visit unless you're not there.*

GERMAN MYSTIC, ANGELUS SILESIUS (1624–1677)

## Blocks to the Awareness of God's Presence: Idle Wishes, Dreams, Fantasies, Illusions, and Grievances

We are so there. We are so into our heads. We are so into thinking, worrying, analyzing, interpreting, projecting, and judging that we can't see anything except our own projections. There is, therefore, no room for God. We would much rather build our own world than discover God's world. I once went to visit Ken Wapnick for what I think of as a kind of annual spiritual check-up. Ken began our conversation by saying, "How is your Kingdom?" The answer to that question is, "What Kingdom?" If we think we have any Kingdom other than that of God's, we're standing outside the Kingdom.

Only the Will we share with God has the power of creation within it. Idle wishes cannot be shared. Nothing makes idle wishes except idle wishes. Fantasies twist perception into unreality (T-1.VII.3:2). Dreams, fantasies, idle wishes, and grievances are all delaying maneuvers which facilitate dreaming. They are blocks in the awareness of God's presence. God can't come to visit when we are so full of ourselves, so obsessed with thinking that there is no room for God.

We might think of ourselves as two-way radios, capable of both sending and receiving. As it is, we have our tuners set on W.E.G.O. and W.E.G.O. is coming in loud and strong and a little statically—very often with not good news. There is another program being played. We might call it W.G.O.D. We block reception of the voice of God when we identify with our own specialness. We are learning to switch our allegiance from listening to W.E.G.O. to W.G.O.D.

> *God calls you and you do not hear, for you are preoccupied*
> *with your own voice. And the vision of Christ is not in your sight,*
> *for you look upon yourself alone.*

> T-13.V.6:6

As I turn down the volume on W.E.G.O., I begin to realize there is another program being played. I could have been listening to the W.G.O.D. all along. This Voice for God is beautiful, harmonic, and soothing. It speaks to everyone, every moment of every day. It's not that God is not there. I cannot, however, be full of self and fully of God at the same time. Dov Baer (1704–1772), one of the founders of Hasidic Judaism, said, "If you think of yourself as something, God cannot clothe himself in you." Or, as, Menahem Nahum (1730–1797, Ukraine), another of the Jewish mystics, said, "Only one who is nothing can contain the fullness of the Presence." Mindfulness calls for presence where all things are joyous.

> *You may not realize that the ego has set up a plan for salvation*
> *in opposition to God's. It is this plan in which you believe.*
> *Since it is the opposite of God's, you also believe that to*
> *accept God's plan in place of the ego's is to be damned.*
> *This sounds preposterous, of course.*
> *Yet after we have considered just*
> *what the ego's plan is, perhaps you will realize that,*
> *However, preposterous it may be, you do believe in it.*

W-71.1:1–4

## G.P.S.: God's Plan for Salvation

The ego's plan is to keep us safe in a hidden secret room, a place of isolation inside a mind carefully concealed inside a body. The Holy Spirit is the only guidance system which can bring us Home. I can make a conscious choice, accept guidance as a way of life, and make a living connection with God's Plan for Salvation; or, I can follow the ego's program, the program of the world, the program of consensus reality, habit, convention, hearsay, and gossip. In this way, I will find only the world, only the external, only that which I project onto the world.

If you have a G.P.S. in your car or you have ridden in a car with someone who has a G.P.S., you know how it works. A small black box sits on the dashboard of the car. Into the little black box, we tap in our intended destination. Let's say we want to go home. Within seconds, this little black box makes contact with three different satellites, hundreds of miles away, each moving at 17,000 miles (26,000 kilometers) per hour. Within seconds, it calculates your exact coordinates and beams back the precise information needed to find your destination. Once one's intended destination is set, the G.P.S. will take us there by the straight, fastest way possible, telling us very precisely exactly where to turn, within just a few feet of our needing to make that turn.

> *To change your mind*
> *means to place it at the disposal of true Authority.*

T-1.V.5:6

## Recalculating

If we're going down the road using a G.P.S. and we decide to pull off to get gas, or maybe we want to stop for lunch along the way, the moment we turn off our intended destination, the G.P.S. will begin saying, "recalculating, recalculating." The Holy Spirit is our G.P.S. Coming into this world, a path is laid out for us—leading us directly Home. As with all children, our basic problem is the authority problem. We say to God—"Thank you very much, God. I would rather do it myself." And then we go off to construct our own fantasy worlds—our own little kingdoms.

Adam hides in the bushes; Moses goes off into the desert; Jonah gets on a ship and heads out to sea; we each find various ways of running away and not paying attention, of doing anything other than what God is asking us to do with our lives. We become instead self-absorbed. We get caught up in our stories and lose sight of the bigger plan that God has laid out for us.

> *The issue of authority is really a question of authorship.*
> *When you have an authority problem,*
> *it is always because you believe you are the author of yourself*
> *and project your delusion onto others.*

> T-3.VI.8:1–2

Like a recalcitrant child refusing to follow the guide of a wise parent, we simply do not believe that if we followed the guidance of the Holy Spirit we would get the results that we *want*. After all, we want what we want; so, how could we get the results we want if we follow a Voice other than that of the ego? Jesus says, "Straight is the way and narrow is the path which leads to life and few there are that go therein. Broad is the way and wide is the path that leads to destruction and many there are that go therein" (Matthew 7:13–14). Though a straight path is set before us, we also have free will and the ego is anxious to be in control, so we're going along and we think— "He's cute. I think I'll chase after him for awhile." And then we go, "Oh my God, divorce" or "Oh good Lord, bankruptcy!" And, instantaneously, God's Plan for Salvation goes, "recalculating, recalculating." Lesson 49 from the Workbook is, "God's Voice speaks to me all through the day." God's Voice is always there, always providing guidance. The question is, am I willing to listen or shall I wait for some crash and burn experience to wake me up. Or, can I demonstrate a willingness to learn, day-by-day, what is needed in order to bring my mind in line with the guidance of the Holy Spirit.

> *The curriculum is highly individualized, and all aspects*
> *are under the Holy Spirit's particular care and guidance.*

> M-29.2:6

We go through different terrains of biology-time and culture; and yet, there are overlaps and similarities because our psychologies are similar even though the landscape is different. We walk down different paths, over different hills, and find our way through different valleys; and yet, the closer we get to Home, the more we realize there is but one road we walk along.

Jesus frequently uses the analogy of gardening in his parables as he does when he says, "The Kingdom of Heaven is like a grain of mustard seed." Seeds are tiny information packets containing all the information needed to turn an acorn into an oak, or a pine nut into a mighty fir. We can use this tendency toward automatic guidance. Living the Course, we begin to grow naturally toward God (W-71.5:1). God's Plan for Salvation works simply because, by following His direction, we seek salvation where it can be found—not in a dream, not in a fantasy, but right here, right now in alignment with Heaven. The question is—do I have my G.P.S. turned on? Am I listening to the programming that comes from W.E.G.O? If I do, then it's for sure I'm lost.

> *If you listen to the wrong voice you "have" lost sight of your soul.*
> *You cannot lose it, but you can not know it.*
> *It is therefore "lost" to you until you choose right.*

> T-5.II.7:12

## Peace and Understanding

Modern brain research suggests that the more we exercise our brains, the longer we are able to put off senility. Listening to the Holy Spirit takes practice but as with any exercise, the more anyone does it, the easier it gets. Listening to Spirit, I more easily notice when temptations to fall into ego arise. I can then more easily also say, "No, thank you," and make the choice to do the right thing. How do I know if I have the right answer? I know if the answer brings me peace. Peace and understanding go hand-in-hand. They cannot be separate. They are cause and effect to each other.

*If you cannot hear the Voice for God,*
*it is because you do not choose to listen.*
*That you do listen to the voice of your ego is demonstrated by your*
*attitudes, your feelings and your behavior.*
*Yet this is what you want. This is what you are fighting to keep,*
*and what you are vigilant to save.*

T-4.IV.1:1–3

*Everything changes when we change the Inner Teacher.*

DR. KENNETH WAPNICK (1942–PRESENT)

CHAPTER 12

# Why Is This Happening to Me?

## TRIAL, ACCIDENTS, COINCIDENCE, AND DESTINY

*Whatever aspect of the soul we neglect,*
*becomes a source of suffering.*

THOMAS MOORE

## "God! How Could You Do This to Me?"

The only survivor of a shipwreck washed up on a small, uninhabited island. He prayed feverishly for God to rescue him. For days he scanned the horizon but he saw nothing. With a piece of broken glass and a bit of dried tinder, he was finally able to start a fire. And, he eventually managed to build a little hut to protect him from the elements and to store a few possessions. One day, while he was scavenging for food, some embers caught the hut on fire and he arrived at his home to find his little hut in flames with smoke rolling up to the sky. The worst possible thing had happened. Everything he had was lost. He was stunned with disbelief, grief, and anger. He cried out, "God! How could you do this to me?" The next day, he was awakened by the sound of a boat approaching the island! "How did you know I was here?" asked the weary man. "We saw your smoke signal," came the reply.

The problems people bring me sometimes find expression in terms of, "Why is this happening?" as though some cosmic force was behind everything. Emperor philosopher Marcus Arelius said, "All things happen as they should." That is after all, the way they happen. In everything, even little things, things which seem insignificant or do not make sense at the time, there is a plan. *The script is written* (W-158.4:3). Our passage through space and time is not an accident. It is not without design. A young man told me about an experience he had while he was doing a job he hated. He stopped the van he was driving and started banging his head on the steering wheel saying, "Why is this happening to me?" and then he heard, "To prepare you for the rest of your life." Another man told me of being a passenger in a car, which was heading directly into a collision with the side of a truck and he heard, "Don't worry. This has to happen. Everything will be okay." What is interesting about this second passage is the second sentence. "This has to happen."

> *Some of your greatest advances you have judged as failures,*
> *and some of your deepest retreats you have evaluated as success.*

T-18.V.1:6

We've all had the experience of having something happen and then saying: "I would never have chosen this." When I lost a country inn I owned in 1989, left the Methodist ministry, and lost nearly everything I had, financially speaking, I asked, "Why is this happening?" I later realized that was what had to happen. I had to go through this crash and burn and I had to step away from the Methodist ministry in order to gain perspective. I had "chosen" this experience and it was necessary to go through this purification to experience life at a deeper level. In 2001, dealing with cancer and the possibility of death enabled another even deeper letting go. The only way ahead was to accept the very real possibility of imminent mortality which again forced me into the moment. Living in the moment always miraculously brings everything to life.

> *Being responsible I see*
> *My past was the only one that could be.*
> *I could not have done it differently.*
> *And so from guilt, I am set free.*
> *No nostalgia, no remorse.*
> *There really was no other course.*

## The Past As Well Held No Mistakes

Given all the possible factors of heredity, environment, economics, and faith, each of us walks the face of this earth as best we can and God never condemns our stumbling along the way. Forgiveness of ourselves lies in the acceptance of the fact that we could not have a different past. It was what it was, and the best thing we can do is to release it for correction and leave it in the past.

> *The time will be as right as is the answer.*
> *And this is true for everything that happens now or in the future.*
> *The past as well held no mistakes . . .*

M-4.VIII.1:4–6

The further we are along the path, the more we can look back and see it was perfect for what we needed to learn. The presence of our parents or the lack thereof was precisely what was needed for our spiritual development. The place we grew up in was the right place. What I'm going through at the moment is a part of my life's lessons. I'm laying in a hospital bed, I'm facing bankruptcy, my wife is leaving me, I have cancer, whatever it is, there is great strength in loving what is.

*Your passage though time and space is not at random.*
*You cannot but be in the right place at the right time.*
*Such is the strength of God. Such are His gifts.*

W-42.2:3–6

When everything is falling apart, something else is trying to be born and accepting responsibility for what is happening helps me deal with it. We are not driven by external, purposeless events. Everything is a part of our spiritual journey; after all, it is what we are experiencing. No accidents are possible in the Universe as God created it and every accident is a lesson. There is a French proverb which says that we often meet our destiny on the road we took to avoid it. We are constantly learning and the older we get, the more we know that life itself is something which goes far beyond the mundane, the body, and everydayness.

*Life can only be understood backwards,*
*but it must be lived forwards.*

DANISH THEOLOGIAN SOREN KIERKEGAARD (1813–1855)

## Assuming Responsibility

A study done in the late 1990s on people who had lived to the age of one hundred tried to determine if there were any psychological conditions which had enabled them to live so long, outside of the obvious physical conditions which prevailed. Anyone who has lived to the age of one hundred has seen a lot and has inevitably been through a lot of pain and distress. The thing they found that all of them had in common was the ability to successfully handle stress.

*My barn having burned to the ground I can now see the moon.*

The Chinese symbol for *crisis* has a dual meaning: *danger* and *opportunity*. The Japanese word for *thank you* is *arigato,* which means *hardship exists.* According to the wisdom of the East, things turn into their opposite; out of hardship, good fortune will follow.

*There is a time for expanding and a time for contraction;*
*one provokes the other and one calls for the return of the other.*
*Never are we nearer the light, than when darkness is deepest.*

INDIAN SPIRITUAL TEACHER SWAMI VIVEKANANDA (1863–1902)

The place in which we need to let go is really very clear to us if we want to admit it. Letting go is sometimes the only solution and the best solution. It is not my guilt which makes me suffer. It's holding on to guilt which give me pain. Pain is the only sacrifice the Holy Spirit asks (T-19. IV.(B).3:7). As the deaf/blind American author Helen Keller (1880–1968) expressed it, "Although the world is very full of suffering it is also very full of the overcoming of it." When we hear of someone who has gone through some difficulty or has perhaps been born with a disability and has gone ahead to live to the fullest despite that difficulty, we cannot help but be impressed with the power of the Mind. Helen Keller was left blind and deaf at 19 months of age as a result of scarlet fever. Despite her severe disability, with the aid of her teacher, Anne Sullivan, Helen graduated from Radcliff and she wrote twelve books. The title of her autobiography, *Light in Darkness*, says it all. Keller once said, "I thank God for my handicaps, for through them, I have found myself, my work, and my God." Can we say that we are grateful for our handicaps or our hardships? Do we know how much they have helped lead us back home again to God?

*Trials are but lessons that you failed to learn presented once again,
so where you made a faulty choice before you now can make a
better one, and thus escape all pain that what you chose before has
brought to you. In every difficulty, all distress, and each perplexity
Christ calls to you and gently says, "My brother, choose again."*

T-31.VIII.3:1–2

## Shake it Off and Step Up

A farmer owned an old mule that fell into a well. After carefully assessing the situation, the farmer sympathized with the mule, but decided that neither the mule nor the old well were worth the trouble of saving. He called his neighbors together and told them what had happened and enlisted their services to haul dirt to bury the old mule in the well and put him out of his misery. Every time a shovel of dirt landed on his back, the mule would shake it off and step up! This he did, shovel load after shovel load. "Shake it off and step up, shake it off and step up. Shake it off and step up!" No matter how painful the shovel loads, or distressing the situation seemed, the old mule just kept right on shaking it off and stepping up! It wasn't long before the old mule, battered and exhausted, stepped triumphantly over the edge of the well!!

## Accidents, Coincidence, and Destiny

No one comes to us by accident. No meeting of any two people is ever unplanned. It does not matter if the encounter lasts one second or a lifetime.

*The simplest level of teaching appears to be quite superficial.
It consists of what seem to be very casual encounters;
a "chance" meeting of two apparent strangers in an elevator,*

*a child who is not looking where he is going running into an adult*
*"by chance," two students "happening" to walk home together.*
*These are not chance encounters. Each of them has the potential*
*for becoming a teaching-learning situation. Perhaps the seeming*
*strangers in the elevator will smile to one another; perhaps the*
*adult will not scold the child for bumping into him; perhaps the*
*students will become friends. Even at the level of the most casual*
*encounter, it is possible for two people to lose sight of separate*
*interests, if only for a moment. That moment will be enough.*
*Salvation has come.*

M-3.2:1–7

In *The Lazy Man's Guide to Enlightenment*, Thaddeus Golas says, "Enlightenment doesn't care how you get there." One of the characters in the movie, *Buckaroo Bonsai* says, "Wherever you go—there you are!" I once counseled someone who said her problems were because she lived in New York. Her problems, of course, had nothing to do with the "state" of the nation. It was all in the state of the mind. We can procrastinate and we can find innumerable excuses for not paying attention. Eventually, we have to face life straight on and deal with what stands in front of us. Eventually, all bills must be paid or forgiven.

*We cannot make a date with enlightenment.*
*Enlightenment is an accident*
*and Spiritual practice makes us accident-prone.*

JAPANESE ZEN TEACHER, SUZUKI ROSHI (1904–1971)

Austrian psychiatrist Victor Frankl, MD, PhD (1905–1997), a neurologist, a Holocaust survivor, and author of the best-selling, *Man's Search for Meaning*, said the people who handled the trauma at Auschwitz best, were those who somehow knew, that even in the horror of this situation, there was some purpose. He said that he found in Auschwitz two types of people. It did not matter what class or ethnic group they were from, there were still two types: decent and loving and non-decent and fearful.

Those who impeccably pursue their destinies are the happiest people, even though they may choose to remain single, turn down wealth, or be crucified. No step that anyone makes along the road is inadvertent. We've already walked this road, so it is a matter of asking the Holy Spirit to help us remember what we already know. In reality, we are Home (Heaven) resting in the arms of God. The story has been played through. We have attained entrance to the Kingdom of Heaven. We are already perfect and whole. We were just dreaming a "silly dream." In Maya's (illusions) house are many mansions. Heaven is reality, not a dream. There is no distress, no sickness, no loss, no bankruptcy, no interpersonal problem, and no death, however extraordinary or mundane that does not come our way holding a gift in its hand.

Everyone has a mission. That mission is to remember what we already know. It's about remembering our true identity, healing our relationships and joining with our brothers and sisters in crossing the bridge to the real world. Those who find a way to fulfill their destinies tell us time and again that they "knew" there was something they had to do. Destiny "had" to be fulfilled, and the best thing was to fulfill it.

# CHAPTER 13

## Self-Observation

### WATCHING, WITNESSING, AND WILLINGNESS

*. . . you are not sufficiently vigilant against the demands of
the ego to disengage yourself. This need not be.*

T-4.IV.6:4

A man hears of a guru who knows three secrets, the three most important things that anyone can know. These secrets will enable him to unlock the mysteries of the universe. He travels over the most difficult of terrains, crossing many rivers, deserts, and mountains. After years of searching, he finds the guru and tells him how long it has taken him and all the difficulties he had to go through and would he now please tell him the three secrets. The guru looks at him and says, "Very well then. 1. Pay attention! 2. Pay attention! 3. Pay attention!" According to American psychiatrist Dr. David Hawkins (1927–present), spiritual devotion is a continuous inner lifestyle that incorporates constant watchful awareness.

Course student/teacher Pamela Silberman, author of *Simply Being*, applies this principle of watchful awareness in terms of the old children's game called, "I Spy." "I spy an attack thought. I spy myself being judgmental. I spy a belief in specialness. I spy myself slipping into guilt." With this game, we can observe every story we want to tell ourselves about the world. Once we see the game, we are then in a position where we can more easily let it go—we do nothing. We simply do not play into the silly game.

## Watching and Wallowing

Watching the mind from a detached position can be done with composure and serenity. Watching is different than wallowing. Seeing the mind means developing some control over it. We are then no longer simply reactionary. When some difficulty comes up, we can ask ourselves, "What is this for? What purpose does it serve? How am I to respond?" Shall I rely on old buddies like guilt and fear, attack, and defense, or is there a better way?

*Everyone here has entered darkness. . .*

T-25.III.6:1

## Hiding in the Shadow

There is a story about a Middle Eastern traveler who was sleeping one night in his tent. He began to get hungry and started thinking about the bag of dates he had in his satchel. He turned on his flashlight and dug into his bag of dates and noticed that the first one had a worm in it, so he threw it away. The second date had a worm in it, so he threw that one away. The third date had a worm in it, so he threw that one away. At this rate, he would soon have no dates left so he turned off the light and ate the rest of his dates. Like the traveler who ate the dates filled with worms, it is easy to pretend that the problem isn't there.

*Something equivalent to the solitude of the*
*wilderness is an essential part of mystical education.*

ENGLISH AUTHOR AND MYSTIC EVELYN UNDERHILL (1875–1941)

We have so much resistance to enlightenment that reaching it is not an easy process; after all, the ego wants to do things the way it wants to do it; and, it is very attached to its identity as a personality and a body in the world. It took many years of searching, meditation, and struggle before the Buddha reached enlightenment. Mohammed also went through a difficult process of inner reflection before his awakening. Jesus's ministry is prefaced by his forty days and forty nights in the wilderness where he goes through a series of grueling temptations by the devil (the ego). The three temptations put before Jesus are descriptive of American psychologist Abraham Maslow's (1908–1970) hierarchy of needs: 1) the need to satisfy the body, (turn stone into bread); 2) the need to show off, (throw yourself off the temple); and 3) the thirst for power (all these kingdoms of the world can be yours). All are typical ego temptations—and what is Jesus's response—"Get thee behind me Satan." Satan is the great *separator*, the great *divider*. Satan is that part of our mind which makes us think we're special.

*Look straight at every image that rises to delay you,*
*for the goal is inevitable because it is eternal.*

T-12.II.5:6

This world is a hiding place from God. Being preoccupied with the body and our position in the world, it is easy to become more interested in the externals than the infinite within. All the while, there remains the feeling that "something" is missing. We long for Home. We long to return to our source; and yet, we're persistently distracted.

## Don't Go Back to Sleep!

In living the Course, it may look as though things are getting worse rather than better. We each have a lot of stuff buried in the cellar of unconsciousness and as we begin to clean house and begin to remove our projections and realize that "they are our projections," as we begin to accept responsibility for the confusion we find around us, the scene can be depressing. But, fear not and do not give up. Remember, it is the ego which is frightened and you are not an ego. Don't throw the book in the wastebasket. Don't stop doing the work.

In the Gospels, Jesus asks us to be vigilant, alert, attentive, and observant. According to traditional Christianity, we are to watch out for the devil and the enemies of God. God, however, has no enemies. We are easily seduced into unconsciousness, fantasy, sleep, and dreams; and, we do not realize how much we rely on habits for direction and idols for rewards. We are highly vigilant for our idols (our own gods)—the way we look, how much money we have, the car we drive, or our status in the community. Yet, we lack vigilance for the things of God (truthfulness, gentleness, open-mindedness, tolerance, etc.). We can, however, be just as vigilant against the ego's demands, as we are for them.

## The Pitiful Abyss of Meaninglessness

The ego was not formed in a day and it's not going to go away quickly. We should be glad that we will not be *hurled* into reality. The unwinding of the knots of complexity of the ego can be a most difficult process. The ego is a trickster. It may persuade me that I have mastered some part of the Course; and then, I find when tested that I've only given lip service to it and I need to take it deeper. We do not realize how much guilt we have buried until we begin to look at it; and, we should not be surprised to hear that the closer we get to purified perception, the more frightened the ego becomes.

*A human being has so many skins inside, covering the depths*
*of the heart. We know so many things, but we don't know ourselves!*
*Why, thirty or forty skins or hides, as thick and hard as an ox's*

*or bear's, cover the soul. Go into your own ground*
*and learn to know yourself there.*

GERMAN MYSTIC, MEISTER ECKHART (1260–1326)

Freud said that in order to experience wholeness, we need to make the unconscious conscious. He said of his own self-analysis that it "was like looking into a dung heap." As I begin to pull away the layers of guilt, I find more guilt underneath; and yet, I must be willing to look at this darkness not to confirm its reality. I look at it in order to see that: "Nothing real can be threatened. Nothing unreal exists. And herein lies the peace of God" (T-in.2–4).

In *Shambhala: the Sacred Path of the Warrior*, Chogyam Trungpa Rinpoche tells the story of traveling with his teacher and a group of other monks. As they approached a temple, a large vicious dog tied up outside the temple began to bark at them, yanking at his chain. Suddenly, the chain broke, and the terrified monks ran in horror. As Rinpoche ran, he looked back, and saw his Master holding out his hand and pointing downward as a command for the dog to stop. The dog put its tail between its legs, and went back to his place near the temple. After the monks returned to their teacher he said, "Always, always run at the fire." As they proceeded into the temple, the dog lay docilely, nearby. Running away only deepens dread. Looking the devil in the face is crucial in the undoing of the "seeming power" of the ego. Open that letter from the IRS. Listen to your doctor. Listen to your body, your wife, your child, your boss. I have to be willing to go into the cave of darkness. I cannot run away. I cannot hide. Every hero or heroine comes eventually to face themselves. Delay only adds on unnecessary pain.

As the body is not cleansed with one cup of detox tea, one fast, or one colonic, so I may come to a moment of clarity only to find it fade away; and, unwilling to continue watching my thoughts, I may be seduced back into sleep. Awakening comes not in just one moment of clarity. Just as I continue to exercise to keep my body in shape, so can the soul be "exorcised" by a continued willingness to be vigilant. It is, thus, that we have 365 lessons in the Course all slowly leading us ever closer to the memory of God.

*Again and again have you attacked your brother,*
*because you saw in him a shadow figure in your private world.*

T-13.V.3:6

## Who Knows? Only the Shadow Knows

On a day-to-day basis, we know more of darkness than the light because darkness is where we hide. This darkness, lurking within, was described by Swiss psychiatrist Dr. Carl Jung (1875–1961) as the shadow, an unconscious complex, containing the repressed (intentionally forgotten) aspects of consciousness. The shadow represents a "knot" in the psychic system. We see these knots in slips of the tongue and behaviors that are "out of character" or hard to account for. Alcoholism, drug addiction, depression, anxiety, obsessive-compulsive behavior, laziness, tiredness, and anger are all manifestations of the shadow. The shadow is slippery. It represents things I do not want to acknowledge in myself, though I see it easily in others.

*Everyone carries a shadow, and the less it is embodied in the*
*individual's conscious life, the blacker and denser it is.*
*At all counts, it forms an unconscious snag,*
*thwarting our most well-meant intentions.*

SWISS PSYCHIATRIST DR. CARL JUNG (1875–1961)

Mark Twain once said that nothing was quite as satisfying as the failure of a friend. You have to love Mark Twain for his irreverence and his keen ability to call a thing from the ego perspective. Have you ever heard about someone's misfortune and then thought, "Now I am ahead of them; now, I have more health or wealth than they do." Did you ever experience jealousy upon hearing of a friend's success? Some folks hear our good news and share it gladly—but not always. The shadow lives in the basement, surfacing when I "act out" or deny I'm in trouble. We see it in over-spending, over-eating, or over-doing anything. The more our unresolved issues (things we don't want to look at) are pushed underground, the more energy it takes to keep them there—the more this "not looking" can drive us crazy. Dr. Carl Jung describes how in therapy one day, a forty-five-year-old patient suddenly blurted out: "But I could never admit that I wasted the last twenty-five years of my life!" Until we look at the shadow, we're at its mercy. Not until we look at this darkness are we able to dissipate some of the ego's energy.

*Your ego is smarter than you are, way smarter,*
*and if you don't recognize that and respect it,*
*you stand very little chance against it.*

JED MCKENNA (*SPIRITUAL ENLIGHTENMENT: THE DAMNEDEST THING*)

While teaching in Sing Sing, I had a prisoner tell me that he was glad that he got caught, as he simply could not keep running, hiding, and acting out forever. The only way out was getting arrested. In the movie *Frost/Nixon*, it was clear that Nixon eventually had to tell the truth. The constant denial became a great burden to him. As hard as it was for him to confess it, living with the lie was even worse than admitting to what the world already knew.

## Egg in My Beard

Ram Dass, formerly Dr. Richard Alpert (1931–present, U.S.), one-time professor of psychology at Harvard University, ventured off to India in 1967, where he met Neem Karoli Baba, who became his guru; and in time, Ram Dass became himself a spiritual teacher. Several years after his own awakening, Ram Dass met a woman who had also taken on the role of guru with a number of her own disciples. She had been a housewife from Queens, New York. One day, while relaxing in the bathtub, she had an awakening that led to her expounding her philosophy. When she and Ram Dass met, it was electric. The two of them combined forces and began to lecture in tandem. Ram Dass and his associate were teaching celibacy as part of the process of reaching higher awareness. Yet, they were themselves no longer celibate. Fortunately, Ram Dass is an honest man and he could not go on for long in this condition and he acknowledged the mistake in a delightful article titled, *Egg in My Beard.*

We, each of us, get egg in our beards—our slips show. We pick our nose in the "privacy" of our car and then notice someone is watching us. We have a little too much to drink at a party and try to pretend we're okay. We become addicted to some negative habit and struggle to break it. We make mistakes. We get fat and struggle to lose the weight. We go into debt and then it seems we cannot get out. Living the Course, we allow our brothers and sisters to have egg in their beards, or whatever it is that's strange about one's individual psychology without letting it take us off balance. We then go ahead and love despite seeming defects, divergences, and difficulties—realizing that if we see a problem, that problem resides in our own thinking. If anyone has a problem it can *only* be me.

> *. . . all your dark lessons must be brought willingly to truth,*
> *and joyously laid down by hands open to receive, not closed to take.*

T-14.XI.4:6

It is easier to bury secret thoughts than it is to look at them; and yet in doing so, the ego continues to run, and therefore, ruin our life. We are being asked to go to the root, to the center of the knot which begins with our selfishness, and thus, our separation. In this sense, the Course is not easy but the reward of light and love that comes with the demonstration of willingness to look at our shadow is oh-so-rewarding. Despite the level of darkness, every experience is important in spiritual growth and we never know how misfortune may lead to fortune. Failure often comes at the hour of deepest darkness which precedes the dawning of the day of success. Freedom from ego requires perseverance, alertness, and a willingness to stay awake. Once we have demonstrated our willingness to face any problem, and be honest about our part in misperception, things change. In order for a tree to grow tall, its roots must go deep.

The following are a few shadowy tricks of the ego. Watching out for these tricksters, we can take things to a higher level, deeper level. Deeper because we have removed some of the blocks to the awareness of loves presence; higher because we are now freer than before.

## Watch for Lying and Hiding (Denial)

Denial is the most subtle, and therefore the trickiest of the defenses. It is often easier to come to terms with our enemies than it is with ourselves. Projection is "out there." It's "clear" why we are mad. We can probably come up with a list of reasons. It's not always so clear when we are in denial; after all, one of the qualities of denial is to deny being in denial. It is not necessary to bring out all of one's dirty laundry and hang it up for the world to see. That would not be truly pleasant or helpful for the world or for us. What we are being honest with is ourselves. What we hide is nothing, but we do not know that as long as we "cherish" our secret sins and hidden hates. Not only do we watch and witness; we must go further and accept our part in the dreaming of the world, and willingly relinquish our role as guardian of the ego.

> *The escape from darkness involves two stages:*
> *First, the recognition that darkness cannot hide.*
> *This step usually entails fear.*
> *Second, the recognition that there is nothing you want*
> *to hide even if you could. This step brings escape from fear.*
> *When you have become willing to hide nothing,*
> *you will not only be willing to enter into communion*
> *but will also understand peace and joy.*

T-1.IV.1:1–5

## Watching for Embellishment and Elaboration

When temptation arises to lie about even small things, an exaggeration, some embellishment, overstatement, or understatement about how hard we work, or how much money we spent, or how we were mistreated ask: "Why would I want to engage in an embellishment? Do I really need to go there?" What would want to exaggerate or elaborate, except the ego? When asked a question, can I answer as truthfully as possible? Why do we sometimes say, "I'll be honest with you"? Does that mean that at other times we are not being honest? It's important to feel (be) clean. The soul, by nature, loves clarity. Cleanliness makes things look beautiful. A receptive mind is conflict free.

> *Do you prefer that you be right or happy?*

T-29.VII.1:9

1. **It is not necessary to be right.** It can actually be more refreshing to be wrong. The truth is going to come to the fore, so I might as well open the door. Speak the truth, take a deep breath, and trust God. Then we feel even better, happier because we are also freer. Remember separation is our greatest problem. We want to feel connected. When I was a graduate student, I was taking a class in group therapy so that we students could run such groups someday ourselves. Near the end of the term, after we had gotten to know each other pretty well, we were encouraged to go around the room and each share something that we *normally* kept hidden. One man was particularly reticent about this exercise. Finally, it came down to where he was the only one who had not shared and he blurted out, "I killed my wife." There was dead silence in the room as all eyes fell upon him and we listened to his story. As it turned out, he had been driving a car at the time of an accident in which his wife was killed. Though there had been an inquiry into the case, he was not charged with a crime. Still, he felt responsible and he had carried a burden of guilt for many years. He cried and cried and then told us what a relief it had been to have finally shared his awful secret.

2. **Take it to a comrade, companion, loving friend, therapist, or fellow student—someone you love, who loves you, someone you feel you can trust.** Alcoholics Anonymous works in part because people are given permission to say, "I'm an alcoholic," in a warm, trusting, and accepting environment. Tell your mate, who already knows it, that you are an "ego-holic" and she/he might find that refreshing. Openness is always refreshing.

3. **Taking it to the Holy Spirit.** Take it to God. Being truthful means being willing to take responsibility for our
thoughts and our actions—right now. Then we complete
the purification by releasing the actions and thoughts to
Holy Spirit.

*You need but leave the mirror clean and clear of all the images of*
*hidden darkness you have drawn upon it.*
*God will shine upon it of Himself.*
*Only the clear reflection of Himself can be perceived upon it.*

T-14.IX.5:5—7

# CHAPTER 14

# Everyone Has the Answer Now

## Remembering What We Already Know

*Since the Holy Spirit answers truly*
*He answers for all time,*
*which means that everyone has the answer now.*

T-6.IV.3:4

A master received a visit from a professor who wanted to learn about enlightenment. The master poured his guest a cup of tea and kept on pouring while the cup overflowed. The professor saw it and finally could no longer keep quiet. "The cup is overflowing; you can't pour any more into it!" The master replied, "Like this cup, you are overflowing with your ideas. How am I to teach you when you don't have an empty cup?"

*As a man and also one of God's creations, my right thinking,*
*which came from the Holy Spirit or the Universal Inspiration,*
*taught me first and foremost that this Inspiration is for all.*
*I could not have it myself without knowing this. The word "know"*
*is proper in this context, because the Holy Spirit is so close*
*to knowledge that He calls it forth; or better, allows it to come . . .*

T-5.I.4:6–9

## Re-cognizing Truth

Every now and then you'll meet someone who is relatively new to the Course who has taken to it, as we say, "like a duck to water." They begin to get into it right away. This "readiness" comes more from emotional or spiritual preparedness than it does intellect. The Course takes us to a deep "A-ha!" and, therefore, a wholly new way of seeing. It comes in the experience that there is something more than the world we see with our eyes. Eventually, all dreaming ends, all illusions are set aside, and everyone remembers God.

In June of 2007, I contracted encephalitis from a mosquito bite which brought on a temperature of 106 degrees, and produced a grand-mal seizure. I went into a coma, was put on life support, and stayed there for several days. I came out of the coma late at night by myself in a hospital room. I could not talk at first but only stare. I picked up my right hand and brought it around to my face. I then thought, "This is a hand. I wonder how I know what this thing is called." And then a strange thing happened, an inner voice said, "Who wants to know?" I wondered how I knew about language and words. I wondered how I knew about anything; but mostly, I wondered about what it was that was wondering. Everything was fascinating—my hand and the pictures on the wall in the room. Even the next day, seeing my wife Dolores's beautiful face and her gorgeous red hair, everything had about it a wonderful expectant shine. For a little while, the world stopped and I was able to see without *the contamination of interpretation*. There was no past intruding on the present and no bewildering future. Several days went by before I had the thought, "You have bills to pay," "You have to get well." "You have to get out of here." Dolores later said that one of the most amazing aspects of the whole experience was that I stopped planning.

*A healed mind does not plan.*
*It carries out the plans that it receives through*
*listening to wisdom that is not its own.*

W-135.11:1–2

A primary quality of the mystical experience is called the "noetic" quality; noetic means that we come to "re-cognize" or "re-call" something that was already there. Greek philosopher Plato (428 BCE–348 BCE) tells us that the soul is eternal, knows everything, and only has to *re-collect* what it already knows. For Shankara (788–820, India) and Eckhart (1260–1326, Germany), the way of salvation is the way of knowledge or *revelation;* revelation being an intensely personal experience and a direct contact with the transcendent that has nothing to do with words. Revelation transcends time and can happen in an instant. Theoretical physicist Dr. Stephen Hawking (1942–present, England) said his greatest insight into the cosmos came suddenly one evening when he was getting into bed. When revelation came, it came in a flash.

*The ego is the questioning aspect of the post-separation self,*
*which was made rather than created.*
*It is capable of asking questions*
*but not of perceiving meaningful answers,*
*because these would involve knowledge*
*and cannot be perceived.*

T-3.IV.3:1–2

When someone "receives" a poem, they often feel that it has been given to them. Saint Hildegard of Bingen (1098–1179, Germany) and Saint Teresa of Avila (1515–1582, Spain) both said they received their books in an instant. Amadeus Mozart (1756–1791, Germany) said he would receive (hear) an entire sonata in an instant. It was not a matter of *composing.*

In the same way, the Course was *given* to Helen. It was just a matter of putting it down on paper. No "composition" was called for. Vision enables us to know what we have all already seen, not in time but eternity. The Holy Spirit's teaching is, thus, a lesson in our *re-membering, re-collecting, re-cognizing,* or putting back together again what spirit already knows.

> *We are not concerned with intellectual feats nor logical toys.*
> *We are dealing only in the very obvious, which has been overlooked*
> *in the clouds of complexity in which you think you think.*
>
> W-39.1:3–4

In *The Critique of Pure Reason* of 1781, German philosopher Immanuel Kant (1724–1894) posited the existence of two kinds of knowledge, *a priori* knowledge and *rational* knowledge or reason. The intellect is based on information, facts, and associations gathered from life. That which is *a priori*, we intuitively know to be true. Everyone knows, for example, that there is such a thing as "love," though there is no "form" of the thing in the world. We must then go beyond the mind to get to the Mind, to Knowledge, and thus, to Being.

> *Rationality can take you only so far.*
>
> ENGLISH TAOIST WEI WU WEI (1895–1986)

Ji-Un, a Singon master, was a well-known Sanskrit scholar. When he was young, he used to deliver lectures to his brother students. His mother heard about this and wrote him a letter. "Son, I do not think you became a devotee of the Buddha because you desire to turn into a walking dictionary. There is no end to information and commentary, glory, and honor. I wish you would stop this lecture business. Shut yourself up in a little temple in a remote part of the mountain. Devote your time to meditation and in this way attain true realization."

To find out what is "really going on," it's not necessary to take in any more information. We are all suffering from information overload and the information we've been given is all about the world. To find out what is really going on, we need to turn to the beyond within. Go out into the desert, sit down, and wait. Or, more appropriately, as Jesus says in the Gospels, "Go into the closet and shut the door and pray to your Father who is in secret" (Matthew 6:6). In other words find a quiet place—sit down and wait and after a while, it is possible to have some idea of what is really going on. When we stop thinking (which stops the world), we find out what is really going on.

## Perception Rests on Choosing.

Everything in this world is a matter of choice. Knowledge which precedes time and perception is not a matter of choosing. It is rather a simple matter of Being. Perception is uncertain. Though we all *know* better, we perceive the sun going around the earth. I see my friend at a distance in the shopping mall. As I approach, I see it's someone else. Perception has not given me the correct information. When we see a house from one side, we "make up" the other sides. I assume that the other sides are there. If I'm watching a movie, I may see only a façade, or I might see a landscape projected onto a screen behind the actors. Is there something *there* in a dream? We do not know how projective we are until we stop projecting. A new student, after a few weeks of working with the Course, came to me and said, "I'm beginning to realize how incredibly judgmental I am." And I said, "That's great! You're getting it."

*Yet projection will always hurt you.*
*It reinforces your belief in your own split mind,*
*and its only purpose is to keep the separation going.*

*It is solely a device of the ego to make you feel different*
*from your brothers and separated from them.*

. . . .

*The ego uses projection only to destroy your perception*
*of both yourself and your brothers.*

T-6.II.3:1–3 & 7

Not long before he died, Swiss psychiatrist Dr. Carl Jung (1875–1961) was interviewed by Sir Laurence Vander Post (1906–1996, South Africa) for the BBC, in London. Near the end of the interview, there is this wonderful moment when Dr. Vander Post asks Dr. Jung if he believes in God. Jung pauses for a moment and then says, "Believe in God? No, I know." When we know, questions cease. Belief is weak, uncertain. Beliefs can change. Knowing is sure.

Knowledge is *a priori*. It is timeless. It is wordless. It is certain. It is not divided. It is beyond subject and object. Subject and object means "self" and "other." Knowing is a direct experience of Being. Knowing is Oneness. Only oneness is free of conflict (T-3.VIII.6:8). Knowing is a deep and profound insight into essence. It is stable, unchanging, and conflict free. It is not bodily or sensuous.

*You do not need judgment to organize your life,*
*and you certainly do not need it to organize yourself.*
*In the presence of knowledge*
*all judgment is automatically suspended,*
*and this is the process that enables*
*recognition to replace perception.*

T-3.VI.3:5–6

## Labeling

Zen Buddhism speaks of a state of mind beyond thought and "no-thought." It is a state in which the labeling of things has ceased. As Zorba, the Greek, says to his wealthy American companion while dancing on the beach in Crete, "There is only one thing wrong with you boss! You need a little madness!" In order to see, we've got to be free of rigid, egoistic thinking. A Shinto priest, when asked about his theology, told journalist Bill Moyers, "I don't think we have a theology. We dance."

*When you love someone you have perceived him as he is,*
*and this makes it possible for you to know him.*
*Until you first perceive him as he is you cannot know him.*

T-3.III.5:3

It says in Genesis that Adam *knew* Eve. When we love someone, we see them as they are. We see past the façade; we see their innocence, and for this reason, we love them. We cannot *know* someone when we project onto them. To attack someone is to make them a stranger. When we love, we see the other's wholeness and innocence, which is the only way we can *know* them. This is the way God knows us. I remember looking at Judy, my high school sweetheart, thinking that she could do no wrong. She would not even have known how. She was just purity and innocence. I had the same experience many years later, when I fell in love with my wife, Dolores. Love is not something we can figure out. Loving is remembering Oneness.

*A memory that is not alive to the present does not*
*"remember" the here and now, does not "remember"*
*its true identity, and is not memory at all.*

AMERICAN CATHOLIC MYSTIC, THOMAS MERTON (1915–1968)

The memory of God is impossible for the ego. God does not know of the ego as God knows us only as Self, only in truth—not in our dreams—not as an illusion. An illusion is an illusion. If God is real, the ego is not. If the ego is real, God is not. The Holy Spirit is the bridge between perception and knowledge. By using perception in such a way that it reflects knowledge, we remember God.

> *Take paradox from the thinker and you have a professor.*
>
> SOREN KIERKEGAARD

## Paradox

According to D. T. Suzuki (1870–1966, Japan), the man who brought Zen Buddhism to the West, knowledge cannot be described as it stands *above* or *outside* of the boxes of words and reason. According to Suzuki, "When language is forced to be used for things of the transcendental world, it becomes warped and assumes all kinds of oxymora and paradoxes." Satori, the spiritual goal of Zen Buddhism, is an experience free of concepts. The Course is likewise filled with paradox:

- Use the Mind to go beyond the mind.
- We *overlook* what is not there.
- To say, "Of myself I can do nothing" is to gain all power.
- We forgive what no one ever did.
- A miracle is the doing of undoing, or the undoing of doing.
- If you want to see—close your eyes.
- Matter does not matter.
- Awakening is rest.
- Death is nothing.
- As we forgive the world our guilt—we are free of the world

- To find yourself—lose yourself.
- What we thought we were seeking is seeking us.
- The best way to get somewhere is to let go of the need to be anywhere.
- Ceasing to be an individual one gains their independence.

## Watching Projection

Watch projection. Just look at it. Try not to analyze or interpret. Just let be what is. Fat, skinny, tall, and short are judgments made with ego eyes. See people instead; see love instead; see innocence. When American Statesman Daniel Webster (1782–1754) wanted to give a person the impression that he remembered him but could not recall his name or where they had met before, he would ask, "How's that old complaint?" Nine times out of ten the person would begin to unfold some grievance, and thereby, identify himself. Living the Course means being willing to look at how much I do not want to see my brother sinless. We want to find problems in the world. Changing vision from the ego's perspective to that of Spirit's is the beholding of a wholly sinless and innocent world. Seeing a sinless world, the love God has for us becomes us. Correct perception simply sees; and in that seeing, there is freedom and knowledge. *Innocence is Truth*. Nothing but truth exists. Truth is all that the innocent see. Selfishness, judgment, complaint, and attack make the world look fuzzy—unclear.

*There is nothing partial about knowledge.*
*Every aspect is whole, and therefore no aspect is separate.*
*You are an aspect of knowledge, being in the Mind of God,*
*Who knows you. All knowledge must be yours,*
*for in you is all knowledge.*

T-13.VIII.2:1–4

A baby was left alone on a blanket in a backyard while the mother ran into the house to answer the phone. When the mother returned, she found that a small non-poisonous snake had crawled onto the blanket and the child, thinking it a toy, had picked up the snake and was shaking it as one would a rattle. The child was safe, and by this time, the snake had been shaken to death. The *innocent of eye* never saw the potential problem. Innocence does not mean naivete. Indeed we need to be very aware of all the tricks of the ego and then choose to see things differently. This requires a reversal in thinking. It means defenselessness instead of defensiveness. It means seeing love in all things even when it looks like an attack.

> *Revelation is literally unspeakable because it is*
> *an experience of unspeakable love.*

> T-1.II.2:7

Choosing God, life is effortless. At any moment of any day, the real us that we are—our true selves—that little spark can choose which direction we will go. If in doubt about a decision, ask: "Will this bring peace of mind, or will it take away my peace of mind?" The decision is right when it brings peace. Repeatedly choose peace, and peace will come.

> *The ego's perception has no counterpart in God, but the Holy Spirit*
> *remains the Bridge between perception and knowledge.*
> *By enabling you to use perception in a way that reflects knowledge,*
> *you will ultimately remember it.*

> T-6.II.7:2–3

> *Perfect vision casts out sin.*
> *It cannot see what is not there.*

## CHAPTER 15

———————

# Healing the T(error)ist Within:

## ON ANGER AND RESPONSIBILITY

*You who feel threatened by this changing world,*
*its twists of fortune and its bitter jests. . .*
*attend this lesson well.*
**The world provides no safety. It is rooted in attack,**
*and all its "gifts" of seeming safety are illusory deceptions.*

W-153.1:1–3 (BOLD MINE)

## The Yenta and the Shenpa:
## Developing Special Relationships

There is an old Jewish saying that being self-absorbed is like "having a Yenta in your cap." *Yenta* is a Yiddish word meaning a blabbermouth or gossipmonger. A Yenta, as in the play and movie, *Fiddler on the Roof,* is also a matchmaker, who *must be* a busybody in order to make a match. A *cap* is one's head. The ego is a Yenta. It likes to tell stories. There is a similar concept in Tibetan Buddhism known as *Shenpa.* A Shenpa is a place where we are "hooked." It is a little irritant that works away at the mind; and after a while, we can't stop thinking about it—letting it go is difficult.

Shenpa, if nourished, can become very strong and powerful. A Shenpa is an addiction to a way of thinking—a (seemingly) justified projection.

> *Healing occurs as a patient begins to hear the dirge he sings, and*
> *questions its validity. Until he hears it, he cannot understand*
> *that it is he who sings it to himself.*
> *To hear it is the first step in recovery.*
> *To question it must then become his choice.*

PSYCHOTHERAPY PAMPHLET 2.VI.1:5–8.

> *These fleeting awarenesses represent the many opportunities given*
> *us literally "to change our tune."*
> *The sound of healing can be heard*
> *instead. But first the willingness to question*
> *the "truth" of the song of*
> *condemnation must arise. The strange distortions woven*
> *inextricably into the self-concept, itself but a pseudo-creation,*
> *make this ugly sound seem truly beautiful.*
> *"The rhythm of the universe," "the herald angel's song,"*
> *all these and more are heard instead of loud discordant shrieks.*

PSYCHOTHERAPY PAMPHLET 2.VI.2:2–6

## Changing Our Tune

A Yenta or a Shenpa can be a grievance we hold in our mind against ourselves or someone else—some little irritant that keeps working away at the mind, convincing us that we are right, someone else is wrong, and we have been hurt by them. Early one Sunday morning while going over my notes for that day's service at a coffee shop in New York City,

I noticed a homeless man sitting directly across from me with a cup of coffee in front of him, talking to himself. There were few people around at the time and he was talking so loudly that by leaning forward and listening carefully, I was able to make out much of what he said. Most people keep their thoughts to themselves. Street folks, however, sometimes let the thought go all the way to the tongue and it finds utterance through the mouth. I could not make out everything he was saying but I got enough of it to know that he was practicing a speech he was going to give to someone in authority—a judge, or a brother, or a sister perhaps. It was clear that he was building a case and defending himself. Did you ever drive around in your car thinking about some Shenpa, building a case for yourself, practicing a speech?

*To interpret error is to give it power,*
*and having done so you will overlook truth.*

T-12.I.1:8

When a Shenpa comes up, it can get in one's face as a test as to whether or not we're there yet. The ego often plays the role of Sneaky Pete; and, just when we think we've gained some freedom from it, it slips in the back door and grabs us. We may think we're judgment free and then we catch ourselves saying something which is blatantly judgmental. Notice the ease with which peace is thrown away. A sales clerk is not as courteous as we would like, our mate does something thoughtless, a little perturbation comes along, someone says something with the wrong intonation, it is taken as an attack and zoom, my peace of mind is gone; and, I am the one who gave it away.

*It is as sure that those who hold grievances will suffer guilt,*
*as it is certain that those who forgive will find peace.*
*It is as sure that those who hold grievances*

*will forget who they are, as it is certain that those*
*who forgive will remember.*

W-68.3:2–3

We may get the foolish idea that if we tell someone off really good once and for all, they will get it and shape up. Let's be clear. It never happens! It never happens because we're attacking another ego. Attack never works. Countering error with error simply provokes fear. How is it possible that in order to make others better, we should first make them feel worse? When we are humiliated or mistreated, does it make us feel like we want to be more cooperative? I would rather have peace of mind than give someone a piece of my mind.

*If you perceive offense in a brother*
*pluck the offense from your mind.*

T-11.VIII.12:1

## Go the Other Way!

If I have a splinter in my finger and it is hurting me, I will "pluck" it out and throw it away. If a thought is hurting the mind, I can take it out and throw it away. I do not deny it or repress it! I just "let it go." There is a wonderful story told about Clara Barton (1821–1914, U.S.), who organized the Red Cross. One time a friend recalled to her a cruel thing that had happened to her some years previously, but Clara seemed not to remember the incident. "Don't you remember the wrong that was done you?" the friend asked. "No," said Clara, "I remember forgetting it. That's all I remember."

*Reason will tell you that the only way to escape from misery*
*is to recognize it "and go the other way."*

T-22.II.4:1

It does not make any difference if I am right or wrong about what I feel hurt or angry about. The mistake is in being angry. When angry, the best advice is always to "wait a minute." The best response is delay. Counting to ten is a good idea and counting to sixty is even better. The ego always speaks first (T-6.IV.1:2). But, it is always possible to suspend the ego projection for a moment in order to gain perspective. Delay means *looking at* what is happening. A Teacher of God cannot be insulted. You cannot be insulted. Only an ego can be insulted and we're not egos. Can you imagine Jesus being insulted? We are to teach no one that they can hurt us. If we do, we teach ourselves that something which is not of God has power over us (T-14.III.8:2).

## Do Not Defend

*No one can become an advanced teacher of God*
*until he fully understands that defenses are*
*but foolish guardians of mad illusions.*
*The more grotesque the dream, the fiercer and*
*more powerful its defenses seem to be.*

M-4.VI.1:6

*Defenselessness is all that is required for the truth*
*to dawn upon our minds with certainty.*

W-135.21:3

While defenses "seem" to protect us from our guilt, fear, and seeming attack of others, they actually make us more insecure and afraid. Ultimately, we stand naked before God. There is no effective attack, blame, or defense to be offered before God against any person. Excuses don't work in Heaven and they don't work here, either. What should you do if someone were to walk up to you and start attacking your body? Do everything in your power to stop them, for three reasons.

1. **We Still Believe that We Are Bodies**
   Proof of that fact is that we are hanging out in bodies. As long as we are hanging out in a body, we will believe that it can be hurt. We would not want our body to be hurt or disabled, so we will do whatever we can to stop someone from hurting it.

2. **We Would Not Want to Facilitate Error in a Brother**
   If we let somebody beat us up, we are being an accessory to a crime. We would not want to be an accessory to a crime. We would not want to be a victim.

3. **We Are not Called Upon to be Martyrs**
   To say, "Do not defend," simply means don't defend the silly ego. It is, after all, a silly ego. It is not who we are. Jesus is standing in front of Pontius Pilate. Pilate says to him, "Do you not hear all the accusations made against you? Don't you have anything to say for yourself?" And, he does not. If Jesus had come back at Pontius Pilate with, "Yes, I really am the Son of God and you're making a big mistake here," we might have questioned whether or not he was the Son of God. Defenselessness does not mean not protecting my body if someone attacks me; permitting destructive behavior; letting others take advantage of us or living under conditions which are abusive.

*Let them be as hateful and as vicious as they may,*
*they could have no effect on you unless you failed*
*to recognize it is your dream.*

T-27.VIII.10:6

## Handling Criticism

What should we do if someone has a criticism of us? Listen! Listen very carefully and ask:

1. Why is this person saying what they are saying?
2. Is there even a grain of truth in what they are saying?
3. Is there some way I might change to make things better?
4. Is there any chance that I can see this differently?

Maybe the other is right. Maybe they are wrong. If they are wrong they need my love. If they are right they need my love. We should also remember that if someone says something bad about us, they are talking about their projection of us. As everything is a projection, there is no reason to take anything personally. We need not be "reactive" if someone has something to say about us that is good or bad. If we are reactive, there must be some "reason" for us to be reactive. Being reactive means I need a better way of seeing. For this reason we need not take too much delight in praise nor should we be too disheartened with blame. In either instance we are seeing ourselves as special.

If my brother is attacking me verbally, valuable information may be coming my way; this person may be telling me something that no one else will. By listening carefully, I come closer to understanding the other and I come closer to a solution. Listening to the criticism will probably be appreciated. This is the real meaning of doing unto others as we would have them do unto us. What others say to me is what I have asked them to say. The only thing ever needing correction is my mind. Seen correctly, I cannot be insulted because there is no "I" to be insulted.

There remains the possibility that the other is wrong. In which case I need to look at why I would be upset if they are wrong. If there is no truth in what is being said, why would I be upset about that which is not true? I watched a bang, bang, shoot 'em up, get in the cars, and chase each other scene on television. All the good guys or the bad guys had to do to get a fight started was to say something about the other guy's mother. Do we not know who our mother is? If something is said against us falsely, this does not mean that we should not say what is true. To respond in anger is always a mistake. All anger is an attempt to make someone else feel guilty (T-15.VII.10:3).

> *Agree with your adversary quickly*
> *while you are in the way with him;*
> *lest at any time the adversary deliver thee to the judge,*
> *and the judge deliver thee to the officer,*
> *and thou be cast into prison.*

MATTHEW 5:25

Not attacking does not mean that we never disagree. It takes skill to be a parent, schoolteacher, counselor, or employer who can deal with difficult situations without anger, attack, spite, or malice. Good teachers never terrorize their students (T-3.I.4:5). Dr. Ken Wapnick writes in *A Course in Miracles and Christianity*: "I have frequently made the public comment that one of the most important lessons a Teacher of God can learn is how to disagree with someone (whether that person be on another spiritual path, or a student of the Course) without it being an attack." Anger keeps the ego alive but anger dissipates when we see we have no need for it.

## Fixing Egos

*The alertness of the ego to the errors of other egos is not the kind of*
*vigilance the Holy Spirit would have you maintain . . .*
*To the ego it is*
*kind and right and good to point out errors and "correct" them. . .*
*If you point out the errors of your brother's ego, you must be seeing*
*through yours because the Holy Spirit does not perceive his errors.*

T-9.III.1:1, 2:1 & 3:1

A little boy wrote a story for his mother and gave it to her. The mother took the story; and, noticing a mistake in grammar, she got a pen and fixed it. She noticed another error and still another error. Finally, she finished fixing the paper and gave it back to her little boy, who was in tears and he said, "I didn't want you to fix it; I wanted you to like it."

It is always a mistake to try and fix another ego. Egos can't be fixed. Egos don't need to be fixed. They don't exist. The world does not need to be fixed. It needs to be loved. Our friends do not need to be fixed. They need to be loved. Our children do not need to be fixed. They need to be loved. The only thing which needs to be fixed is "the cause of the ego" in my mind. There is a *correct form of projection*, namely, the extension of love, and thus, the undoing of guilt through forgiveness. Love is extension. The ego projects to exclude. The Holy Spirit extends to include, and thereby, recognize Oneness.

*. . . attack is never discrete and must be relinquished entirely.*

T-7.VI.1:3

This is heavy teaching. If I see a problem in my brother, it must be in me. To point out error is to amplify error. I have to ask, "What is it in me which needs to find a problem?" With anything I'm about to say I ask: "Will what I'm about to say be truly helpful?" Whenever we attack, we are attacking another ego. How is that ego going to respond? It is going to get angry and defensive, and attack back. Living the Course means listening to criticism, finding the value in it, and thinking about what I might do to see this situation correctly and that 99.9 percent of the time, when we offer up our critiques to others, we're not going to get through to their right mind. We're going to be hitting on their ego and the ego is going to respond the same way egos always have responded—with defense and attack. Thus it is that attack never works and safety lies in defenselessness.

## Let Him Be What He Is

The passage I quote most often in lectures is, "Let him be what he is and seek not to make of love an enemy" (T-19.IV.D.i.13:8). Letting other people be who they are is one of the hardest things for us to do. Thinking we can fix other people means that we think we know "how" to fix them.

> *If you attack error in another, you will hurt yourself.*
> *You cannot know your brother when you attack him.*
> *Attack is always made upon a stranger.*
>
> T-3.III.7:1–3

How many times do I have to get slapped in the face with reality in order to see it? This seeming "Shenpa" thing *which does not exist,* can lead the mind down a mineshaft of righteousness. Anger is an interesting, although not so subtle, response. Where there is smoke there is fire, and even annoyance is a veil drawn over fury (W-21.1:4). If I am in the attack mode, or the complaint mode, even the slightly "annoyed" mode,

I'm blinding myself; and, I've still not learned my lesson. We use a great deal of vigilance to protect our egos; we use very little vigilance in the protection of our right mind.

*You can be as vigilant against the ego's dictates as for them.*

T-4.IV.4:2

There is a story in the Gospel of John (8:1-11) of a woman taken in adultery. According to the Law of Moses, the woman was to be stoned. They bring her to Jesus and ask him what they should do and Jesus says that the one who is without sin should cast the first stone. Beginning with the eldest, they drop their stones and walk away. Jesus then turns to the woman and asks, "Woman, where are your accusers?" To which she says, "Lord, there are none." Jesus then replies, "Neither do I condemn you, go and sin no more." In other words, "Go and do not continue to make the same mistake." It is the eldest who drops the first stone. The longer we've been here, the more we know we have not been able to transition through this world without error.

*Whenever you consent to suffer pain, to be deprived,*
*unfairly treated or in need of anything,*
*you but accuse your brother of attack upon God's Son*

T-27.I.3:1

The ego always speaks first (T-5.VI.3:5). Lesson 6 from the Workbook says, "I am never upset for the reason I think." Therefore, whether my brother is "wrong" or "right" I have to ask the question, "Why am I upset?" Here is a real opportunity for insight. Is there a "glimmer of truth" in the lesson my brother would have me learn?

## You Cannot Be Betrayed, Persecuted, or Crucified

*You have probably reacted for years as if you were being crucified.*
*This is a marked tendency of the separated,*
*who always refuse to consider what they have done to themselves.*

T-6.I.3:1–2

The message of the crucifixion is that it is not necessary to perceive any attack—even the meanest—as persecution. Who I am in truth (Spirit) cannot be persecuted. Spirit cannot be destroyed (T-6.IV.4:1-7). If I act as though I am being persecuted, I place a burden of guilt upon my brothers. If I imprison my brothers, I imprison myself. One of the silliest things anyone could say is, "Look what you made me do now." No one is responsible for how we act or how we feel. Living the Course, I see that I am the *cause* of everything I think and feel. Jesus was whipped, beaten, and placed on a cross to die and he never condemned his accusers. He never projected back.

*Christ left us an example that we should follow in his steps.*
*He did not sin, neither was guile found in his mouth.*
*Who when he was reviled, reviled not again,*
*When he was tortured, he retaliated not*
*but committed himself to Him that judges righteously.*

1 PETER 2:21

If someone acts out of ignorance, they do not know who they are or what they are doing. As my old teacher of transpersonal psychology, Dr. Thomas Hora, used to say, "Ignorance is not a person."

*I could not have said, 'Betrayest thou the Son of Man with a kiss?'*
*unless I believed in betrayal. The whole message of the crucifixion*

*was simply that I did not.*
*The "punishment" I was said to have called forth upon Judas*
*was a similar mistake, Judas was my brother and a Son of God*
*as much a part of the Sonship as myself.*
*Was it likely that I would condemn him when I was ready*
*to demonstrate that condemnation is impossible?*

T-.I.15:5–9

Jesus is hanging on a cross—his body bleeding and dying, a jeering crowd yelling at him, and yet he does not see himself as persecuted. All we are to do is to follow his example in much less extreme cases. We are asked to teach only love in each and every situation, including the times when the world, defined as other people, seems to attack us. If my brother is acting out of fear, it doesn't mean I have to. Just as a parent can look upon a misbehaving child and see past the behavior to the innocence within, so God looks past our misconstruction—knowing the truth of our Being. God has created us perfect. We may be dreaming a dream of imperfection but it is just a dream.

We cannot be hurt and we do not want to show our brothers and sisters anything other than wholeness (T-5.IV.4:4). In the movie *Dead Man Walking*, Sister Prejean, the nun played by Susan Sarandon, did not deny what the criminal, played by Sean Penn, had done. She loved him and looked past his mistakes to the truth that lay within. As we teach, so do we learn; and, if we react as though we are being persecuted, so do we teach persecution. We cannot teach persecution and find inner peace. What we are to teach is our own perfect immunity. We cannot be assailed any more than Jesus was. His is an extreme example. Can we not be more tolerant under much less extreme examples?

*It is not danger that comes when defenses are laid down.*
*It is safety. It is peace. It is joy. And it is God.*

M-4.VI.1:11–15

## The Two Wolves

There is a wonderful Shenpa story from the Cherokee Indian tradition. An old grandfather said to his grandson, who came to him
with anger at a friend, "I too have felt a great hate for those that have taken
so much, with no sorrow for what they do. But hate wears you down,
and does not hurt your enemy. It is like taking poison and wishing your
enemy would die. It is as if there are two wolves inside me. One is kind and
understanding and does no harm. He lives in harmony with all around
and does not take offense. The other wolf is vengeful and full of anger.
The littlest thing will set him into a fit of temper. He fights everyone and
for no reason. He cannot think because his anger and hate are so great.
Sometimes, it is hard to live with these two wolves inside me. Both of
them try to dominate my spirit." The boy looked into his grandfather's
eyes and asked, "Which one wins, Grandfather?" The grandfather smiled
and said, "The one that wins will be the one I feed."

*I thoroughly disapprove of duels.*
*If a man should challenge me, I would take him kindly and*
*forgivingly by the hand and lead him to a quiet place and kill him.*

AMERICAN AUTHOR, MARK TWAIN (1835–1910)

Take all Yenta and Shenpas kindly and forgivingly by the hand to a
quiet place; and there, give it to the Holy Spirit for disposal. And then
walk away and trust that God has done his part. If Spirit wants you to
know the results of the miracle, he will show you. Otherwise, take it on

faith and move along. Experience helps us to recognize a mistake when we make it again. When Shenpa comes, remember: this is a test; it is only a test. Ask Spirit to correct your desire to do it again, and then turn around, walk away, and return again another day when love rules the mind. If I see defensiveness coming up, if I see attack thoughts arising, I know something has gone wrong with my thinking. Our brothers and sisters do indeed sometimes do hurtful things. The question is how do I "see" what has been done? Do I see it as hurtful? Does my ego get plugged in or can I see this as a call for help and take it to a higher level? Do I hit back? Or, can I sit back? We are not to permit abuse. Neither am I to respond with abuse. Those who test us are our best teachers and our friends.

*Those who make you return,*
*for whatever reason to God's solitude, be grateful to them.*
*Worry about the others, who give you delicious comforts*
*that keep you from prayer.*
*Friends are enemies sometimes and enemies, friends.*

SUFI MYSTIC JALALUDDI RUMI (1207–1273)

When any situation is out of our hand, it is time to place it in God's hands. What needs fixing isn't the world; what needs fixing is my perception of the world. Looking at the world with eyes of innocence instead of judgment, we see—we cannot judge. Once we see how the ego plays its games, we realize, "We don't have to play." I need only to ask the Holy Spirit to correct my perception.

*There is a way of finding certainty right here and now.*
*Refuse to be a part of fearful dreams whatever form they take,*
*for you will lose identity in them.*

T-28.IV.2:1–2

## Refuse to Be a Part of Fearful Dreams

It is that simple. If we teach anyone that they can hurt us, we teach ourselves that what is not of God has power over us. We would never attack another unless we believed that they have somehow taken the peace of God from us. If others have the power to take the peace of God from us, we gave them that power.

> *So is the memory of God obscured in minds*
> *that have become illusions' battleground.*
> *Yet far beyond this senseless war it shines,*
> *ready to be remembered when you side with peace.*

T-23.I.12:8–9

## CHAPTER 16

---

# From Selfishness to Self-fullness

### I'm Nobody. Who Are You?

*Selfishness is of the ego, but Self-fullness*
*is of spirit because that is how God created it.*

T-7.IX.1:4

*Prepare you now for the undoing of what never was.*

T-18.V.1:1

Let's review briefly. We think that we are separate, broken off, alone; capable of building our own world and thinking our own thoughts outside of the Mind of God. Our minds are split and while there is a part of us which remembers our Home (Heaven), that is not our everyday experience in this world. Indeed, in our dreaming of the world, we have forgotten that we have a mind which can bring us back to Oneness—a state we never left. We dream that we are an ego caught in a body in space/time and that makes us special.

## The Self Made Man

**Specialness is** the thought of sin made real (T-24.II.3:1). It is a false impression we hold about ourselves and a lack of faith in everyone except ourselves (T-24.VI.1:1). It is a form of self-creations, a function I give myself. It is thinking that I am somehow exclusive, unique, better, or worse than others. Specialness is a concept of self, more highly cherished than truth itself. Specialness is the great dictator of the wrong decisions (T-24.I.5:1). It is the loss of peace. The more I defend my specialness, the less likely I am to be able to hear the Voice for God.

> *You are not special. If you think you are, and would defend*
> *your specialness against the truth of what you really are,*
> *how can you know the truth?*
>
> T-24.II.4:1-2

To see ourselves as special is to think of ourselves as "better than or worse than" others. Either way calls for judgment. We make ourselves special or we make someone else special. We are all equal members of one family, seeking for difference, making ourselves *better than* or *less than* is a form of separation.

Specialness = Sin = Separation = Suffering

Suffering = Specialness = Sin = Separation

Separation = Suffering = Specialness = Sin

Sin = Separation = Suffering = Specialness

## Ways of Being Special

> *Do not forget that any form of specialness*
> *must be defended, and will be.*

PSYCHOTHERAPY PAMPHLET 3.II.10:1

There are myriad ways in which specialness is manifest. We see it most obviously in the search for status and prestige in the world, on our job, in our community, within our family, etc. Let's explore four of the more obvious way specialness may obscure the truth.

> *Your mind is filled with schemes to save the face of your ego,*
> *and you do not seek the face of Christ.*
> *The glass in which the ego seeks to see its face is dark indeed.*
> *How can it maintain the trick of its existence except with mirrors?*
> *But where you look to find yourself is up to you.*

> T-4.IV.1:5–8

### 1.   Egotism: We're Special Because We're Hot

There is a story about four Zen students who decide to go into a week of silent meditation together. They sit down, a couple of hours go by and one of them says, "I wonder if I remembered to turn off the stove." A second one responds, "You fool, you have spoken, and we had agreed not to speak." A third student then says, "What are you thinking about, now you too have spoken." To which the fourth one says, "I am the only one who has not spoken."

> *. . . nothing you do or think or wish or make*
> *is necessary to establish your worth. . . .*

*Your ego is never at stake because God did not create it.*
*Your spirit is never at stake because He did.*

T-4.I.7:6 & 9

Everyone is aware of this particular distortion. We think that we are special because we make lots of money; we drive a fancy car; we are handsome, beautiful, and youthful; we have degrees after our name; we're a VIP. There is certainly nothing wrong with having money, looking and feeling good, etc. None of these things, however, make anyone special; and in them, there is no guarantee of peace of mind. These are external places where salvation may be sought in other people, in possessions, in special situations and events, and the self-concept we seek to make real.

*Do not deceive yourself into believing that you can relate*
*in peace to God or to your brothers with anything external.*

T-1.VII.1:7

Though he was not there at the time, I once stayed in one of the homes of a man who was, at one time, the MVP (Most Valuable Player) in baseball. His mother, who was my hostess, told me that he was a very unhappy man because he was not, that year, on a winning baseball team. As my friend Dr. Scott Olsen so clearly says it, "We must be willing to get rid of all false notions of self. We must be willing to give up all self-created images." The Course encourages us to tell ourselves:

*My salvation cannot come from any of these things.*
*My salvation comes from me and only from me.*

W-70.5:7–8

Me in the above sentences can be understood as me as the Son of God—the Self reconnected with the whole. In Lesson 84, we read the affirmation, "I will worship no idols, nor raise my own concept to replace my Self."

*Routinely, people discover that the life*
*of a celebrity is onerous and burdensome*
*once the novelty has worn off.*

AMERICAN PSYCHIATRIST DR. DAVID HAWKINS (1927–PRESENT)

The more highly defined our position within the world, the more difficult it may be to know the truth, and thus, be free. Famous people (Marilyn Monroe, Elvis Presley, Princess Diana, Anna Nicole Smith, and Michael Jackson) each had a difficult time living in a world, which become for them increasingly artificial. It is said of Marilyn Monroe that she reached "mythic" status. Myth means "not real." Two months before she died, she did a tape-recorded interview for *Life* magazine called, "Marilyn on Marilyn." She talked quite frankly about her feelings concerning the image that had been made of her by Hollywood. She saw this image as a cardboard cutout, a cartoon character. She was clear that it was all a fantasy. Hollywood had created an image of a sex goddess, and it wasn't her. As she expressed it, "I am not a sex goddess, I'm a person." Then she said, in the most poignant way, referring to Hollywood; "And, I let them do it." It was not, however, who she was. She was, she said, and she was crying when she said it, "Just Norma Jean," but Norma Jean had gotten lost in Marilyn Monroe.

## 2.   We're Special Because of Our Opinions

*No one can judge on partial evidence. That is not judgment.*
*It is merely an opinion based on ignorance and doubt. Its seeming*
*certainty is but a cloak for the uncertainty it would conceal.*

W-151.1:1–3

*Nothing is more conducive to peace of mind*
*than not having an opinion.*

GERMAN SCIENTIST GEORGE CHRISTOPH LICHTENBERG (1742–1799)

We may also think of ourselves as special because of the "superior" opinions or attitudes we hold in relationship to each other and the world. Do you know the difference between a crow and a raven? Crows have the four long feathers that come off the tip of their wings. The feathers are called *pinions*. Ravens have five of these feathers instead of four, so it is just a matter of a pinion. Our opinions are just opinions, and therefore, forms of separation. As François-René de Chateaubriand (1768–1848), one of the founders of romanticism in French literature said, "You are not superior just because you see the world in an odious light."

Love makes no comparisons (W-195.4:2). Comparison is an ego ploy. Does "difference" make a difference? Does it matter if we are Republicans or Democrats? Does it matter what church we go to? Does it have anything to do with Heaven?

Kai-Chu, the great Zen teacher, was the head of Tofuki, a cathedral in Kyoto. One day the governor of Kyoto called upon him for the first time. His attendant presented the card of the governor, which read: Kitagaki, Governor of Kyoto. "I have no business with such a fellow," said Kai-Chu to his attendant. "Tell him to go away." The attendant carried the card back with apologies. "That was my error," said the governor as with a pencil he scratched out the words, Governor of Koyoto. "Ask your teacher again." "Oh, is that Kitagaki?" exclaimed the teacher when he saw the card. "I want to see that fellow."

There are no doctors, no captain, no reverends, and no governors in Heaven. There are also no Methodists, no Buddhists, no Baptists, no Hindus, no Muslims, and no Jews. There are no ideologies, no philosophies, or belief systems. That's all stuff we made up.

### 3. Victimhood

We may also think of ourselves as special because of a sorrowful, "victim" condition. "Woe is me. Look at what has happened to me." The Course uncovers a lie hiding inside. We actually like to be crucified. We can all think of individuals who consistently find trouble with the world—ourselves included. The more guilt we carry around, the more we feel punished by external circumstances. Suffering is an emphasis upon what the world has done to injure us. As long as we are victims of something outside ourselves, we cannot see. Furthermore, we are making special the ones we say are persecuting us. Seeing ourselves as persecuted is a convenient way of not looking. If I feel persecuted, then I'm saying that someone else is responsible for the way I feel. It must be you. I point a finger and I say, "I am a good person. You are not."

*My brothers and yours are constantly engaged*
*in justifying the unjustifiable.*

T-6.I.11:4

## The "Whine" of the Month Club

When Country Western singer Hank Williams was asked by a radio disk jockey why he thought it was that he had so many number one hits, Hank said, "Everybody feels good about feeling bad." When I quote that line in public lectures, it always gets a laugh. We laugh because it is true. George Bernard Shaw once said, "When a thing is funny, we should search it carefully for the truth in it." Sigmund Freud wrote a whole book on jokes, realizing the power of the unconscious content of jokes and the truth which often lay behind the joke. Just for fun, here are a few titles from some country western songs, each suggestive of the insanity of the ego:

"My Wife Ran Off With My Best Friend And I Sure Do Miss Him"
"I'm So Miserable Without You, It's Almost Like You Were Here"
"I Liked You Better Before I Knew You So Well"
"How Can I Miss You, If You Won't Go Away?"
"I Keep Forgettin' I Forgot About You"
"If You Don't Leave Me Alone, I'll Go Find Someone Who Will"

The ego *seems to enjoy* being mistreated, abandoned, and betrayed as this is proof that we are *innocent victims* of what other people (the world) has done to us. We all think that we suffer more than other people do which helps us to justify our projections against others. One of the most sobering aspects of the Course is the awareness that, on an ego level, we want to suffer. We actually enjoy wallowing around in our exquisite and most wonderful pain, all of which is proof that we are separate and isolated from the whole. We like being in relationships in which we are abused. We like to tell other people about our problems. We like to talk about our aches and pains as this makes us special and gives us "the right" to complain. When the computer isn't working, when the doctor or the plumber tells me the situation is worse than they thought—what am I to do? Will I see myself as a victim or can I rise above it? If I find myself thinking I am a victim, I can stop and ask "Why?" Asking myself that question creates space in my thoughts and gives me a "choice point"—a point at which it is possible to be free enough from the thoughts and experiences of the moment to choose love (Holy Spirit) instead of fear (ego). The word, *beware,* is used only once in the entire Course and that is in the sentence which says:

*Beware of the temptation to perceive yourself unfairly treated.*

T-26.4:1

The wish to be unfairly treated is a compromise attempt that seeks to combine attack and innocence (T-27.I.1:1–2). The secret of salvation the Course says, lies in the recognition that regardless of what is happening "you are doing it unto yourself" (T-27.VIII.10:1). The "you" that had done this, is the decision-making mind. This is why changing the mind changes everything. The answer to victimhood is the acceptance of responsibility. Accepting responsibility, we cannot project; we cannot blame someone else or our circumstances. Blaming only deepens our sense of guilt. If I really get Lesson 31 from the Course, "I am not a victim of the world I see," I'm going a long way in understanding the whole Course. No matter where we are, no matter what is going on, we are responsible for being here—in this marvelous place—at this marvelous moment.

> *This is the only thing that you need do for vision, happiness,*
> *release from pain and the complete escape from sin,*
> *all to be given you.*
> *Say only this, but mean it with no reservations,*
> *for here the power of salvation lies:*
>
> **"I am responsible for what I see. I choose the feelings**
> **I experience, and I decide upon the goal I would achieve.**
> **And everything that seems to happen to me I ask for,**
> **and receive as I have asked."**
>
> *Deceive yourself no longer that you are helpless in the face of what*
> *is done to you. Acknowledge but that you have been mistaken, and*
> *all effects of your mistakes will disappear.*
>
> T-21.II.2:1–7 (BOLD MINE)

We should be clear that while we are not responsible for what other people do, we are responsible for *how we interpret* what other people do. We can be victims or we can be free.

### 4. We're Special Because We're Spiritual

One of the most subtle means of being special is thinking that we are better than others because we are religious—that God somehow looks with favor upon us in a way that He does not with others. He thus finds us parking spots, tells us how to invest wisely, and gives us strengths others do not have.

Four Catholic ladies are having tea together. One of them takes a sip of tea and says, "My son is a priest, and whenever he walks into the room, all the ladies say, 'Good evening, Father.'" The second lady takes a sip of tea and says, "My son is a bishop, and when he walks into the room, all the ladies say, 'Good evening, your Grace.'" Wow! The third lady takes a sip of tea and says, "My son is a cardinal. When he walks into the room, all the ladies say, 'Good evening, your Eminence.'" The fourth lady takes a sip of tea and says, "My son is a six-foot-two, hard-bodied male stripper. When he walks into the room, all the ladies say, 'Oh, my God!'"

According to *The Tao Te Ching*, if we think we have some knowledge of the Tao and that makes us better than other people, then we are not in tune with the Tao. Thinking one's religion is better than another is a fatal ego ploy. Those who transcend orthodoxy and tradition may think they are better than those who support established institutions. We may think, "I meditate. I'm better than people who don't mediate." Or, "I eat a clean diet. I'm better than people who eat junk food." Or, most insidious, "I'm nonjudgmental, so I'm better than people who are judgmental."

*The self you made can never be your Self.*

W-95.3:3

## I'm Nobody, Who Are You?

So, who are we if we are none of the things mentioned above? A senior minister walks into the chapel of his church, kneels down before the altar, and says, "Lord, I am nobody, I am so nobody." The associate pastor walks by and seeing the senior minister, goes into the chapel, kneels beside him, and he too says, "Lord, I too am nobody, I am so nobody!" The custodian is passing by and, seeing the two ministers on their knees, goes in and also kneels. He too says, "Lord, I too am nobody, I am so nobody!" The associate minister opens his eyes, sees the custodian next to him, hears what he says, taps the senior minister in the side and says, "Look who thinks he's nobody!"

> *Of yourself you can do nothing,*
> *because of yourself you "are" nothing.*
>
> T-8.IV.7:3

Mystics talk about coming to a great void and a deep peaceful emptiness. We might think of the void as the cessation of the ego and an absence of self. It is a peaceful place in which nothing has to happen—where Being can just be. Mystics often speak of themselves as being nobody special. Being nobody special also means the remembrance of the truth of Being; and Being, the Course says is "a state in which the mind is in communication with everything that is real" (T-4.VII.4:3).

> *I'm nobody! Who are you?*
> *Are you nobody, too?*
> *Then there's a pair of us, don't tell.*
> *They'd banish us, you know.*
> *How dreary to be somebody!*

*How public, like a frog.*
*To tell your name the livelong day*
*To an admiring bog!*

AMERICAN POET AND MYSTIC EMILY DICKINSON (1830–1886)

When his friend, Harrison Blake, asked Henry David Thoreau if his adventure by Walden Pond had left him feeling a longing for society, Thoreau answered, "No, I am nothing." Thoreau had gone on retreat to Walden Pond to find himself, that is, to find God within. He could not understand, he said, "all the incessant business going on in Concord." He wrote that in 1845. How much busier and "seemingly" important is today's world? When we stop making up the world, we can see things and enjoy them in their immediacy. There is then no need to change the moment. The mystic is not a projector, and doesn't want to be. As English author Aldous Huxley (1894–1963) expressed it, "Our task is not to be thinking. Our task is to be 'thought.'"

*Why are you unhappy?*
*Because 99.9 percent of everything you think,*
*and of everything you do, is for yourself—*
*And there isn't one.*

ENGLISH TAOIST PHILOSOPHER WEI WU WEI (1895–1986)

When I quote the above from Wei Wu Wei at various lectures, it also gets a nervous laugh. We laugh because we know it is true.

Once at a public dialogue, a man said to the mystic Jean Klein (1916–1998, Austria), "Every time I come to hear you, I notice that you seem so clear and relaxed. You radiate peaceful, loving warmth. You seem happy. Yet, I am always discontent, often stressed out. There are times when I feel quite miserable. What is the difference between us?" Jean said, "You think that you are somebody and I know that I'm not."

## Dropping Personal History

We gain awareness "in the now" by dropping personal history. "If we could erase personal history," says Don Juan, of the Carlos Castaneda books, "we would be free from the encumbering thoughts of others." Don Juan pointed out to his student, Carlos, that he, Carlos, had to renew his personal history daily by telling his family and friends everything he did. If we have no personal histories, no explanations are needed. To express it simply, if you don't have a story, you don't have to fit it. "One day," says Don Juan, "I discovered I didn't need a personal history; so, like drinking, I dropped it."

Don Juan said he knew all kinds of things because:

1. He doesn't have a personal history.
2. He doesn't feel more important than anything else.
3. His death is sitting right there beside him.

If we think of ourselves as special then we may also think that our problems are more important than those of other people. Indeed, the things which establish our individuality in the world are our individual problems. Losing the sense of self-importance, we realize that everyone has the same problem—the experience of feeling separate from God. In describing his mystical experiences, spiritual teacher A. H. Almaas (1944–present) says, "I learn a great deal of what I truly am when I am not trapped in the particulars of personal life and history. I am then the unchanging background witnessing." Or, as spiritual teacher Gangaji (1942–present, U.S.) says it, "I am not bound by the story of me."

*The building of a concept of the self*
*is what the learning of the world is for. This is its purpose;*
*that you come without a self, and make one as you go along.*

*And by the time you reach "maturity" you have perfected it,*
*to meet the world on equal terms, at one with its demands.*
*A concept of the self is made by you.*
*It bears no likeness to yourself at all.*
*It is an idol, made to take the place of your reality as Son of God.*

T-31.V.1:5–7 & 2:1–2

Our bodies come through different terrains of biology, time, geography, and social circumstances; therefore, the form is different but form is only the shell. Content wise, we are all the same. To the ego, if the form looks good, that is the only thing which matters. Form is absolutely irrelevant to spirit and only love is real. The less special we think that we are; the better for sanity. Gaining sanity, we find that what happens to our personal self, our hopes and dreams, our hurts and pains, is not a matter of life and death seriousness. Self beyond selfishness is love. It is formless, spaceless, timeless, infinite, and empty.

Meister Eckhart (1269–1326) used words like *desert* and *barren* to describe his experience of illumination. Spanish mystic St. Teresa of Avila (1515–1582) spoke of the *still wilderness* or the *lonely desert* of the Deity. Yet this is the true country of the soul, a space free from desiring, where the ego cannot reign. While ultimate reality constitutes the true nature of everything, in itself, it is nothing. To be nothing is to discover peace, expansion, and freedom from boundaries. Nothing is full, whole, infinite. It is everything, and it is everywhere. It is omnipresent.

*The self you made is not the Son of God.*
*Therefore, this self does not exist at all.*
*And anything it seems to do and think means nothing.*
*It is neither bad nor good.*
*It is unreal, and nothing more than that.*

W-93.5:1–5

If we succeed in finding release from the prison of individuality, what then? There follows in time another second and yet another second; and, what do we find in that second? We find Oneness. We find the Soul, the Self, Spirit, unhampered by the ego. We are eternity. We are Love. This Self is pure witnessing. It exists prior to time—prior to the big bang and outside of the world of perception. It is not born. It does not die.

I have a friend who takes part in a spiritual practice where people work in dyads, or pairs of twos. Each participant sits facing a partner, and the partners take turns asking each other, "Tell me who you are?" People respond by identifying themselves with their names and their occupations. They may talk about their families and where they live. After they stop talking, the partner asks again, "Tell me who you are?" "I'm so-and-so's wife or husband," etc. Eventually, the participants realize that none of the definitions will do. Who they are in truth then must be that which transcends all of these definitions.

Although the self that we created is not who we are beyond, above, and outside all the illusions of the world, there is a Self that we are in truth. This Self is a holy child made in God's image, not our own. This Self holds the key to inner peace and leads us, once again, Home. Our greatest happiness comes from knowing we are God's child. It comes in doing His will. Lesson 96 from the Course says, *Salvation comes from my one Self.* If there is one Self, there are not two. There is no split mind. There is only oneness.

*I ask you only to stop imagining that you were born,*
*have parents, are a body, will die and so on. Just try,*
*make a beginning—it is not as hard as you think.*

INDIAN SPIRITUAL TEACHER NISARGADATTA MAHARAJA (1897–1981)

*When every concept has been raised to doubt and question,*
*and been recognized as made on no assumptions*

> *that would stand the light, then is the truth left free*
> *to enter in its sanctuary, clean and free of guilt.*
> *There is no statement that the world is*
> *more afraid to hear than this:*
> *"I do not know the thing I am, and therefore do not know what I am*
> *doing, where I am, or how to look upon the world or on myself."*

T-31.V.17:5–7

Holding on to our specialness, our individuality is the thing which makes us separate. We hold on to guilt because it confirms our individual identity.

> *The death of specialness is not your death,*
> *but your awaking into life eternal. You but emerge*
> *from an illusion of what you are to the acceptance of yourself*
> *as God created you.*

T-24.II.14:4–5

It is easier to speak of what we are not than what we are. We are not our bodies, our occupations, our church, our city, state, or nation. We are not our race, our clan, or our families. We are not even our thoughts or that which thinks them, our feelings or that which feels them, because thoughts and feelings which come from the ego are not the truth of our Being. There is a great wisdom as we get older in "learning to die," in letting go of all the accoutrements of things and eminences as valued by the world.

## Oneness Joined as Oneness

*. . . while you think that part of you is separate,*
*the concept of a Oneness joined as One is meaningless.*

T-25.I.7:1

The ego "is" separation and separation is suffering. Oneness is the state we never left. It is endless, timeless, and ours. It is our eternal home. "The memory of God," the Course says "shines not alone" (T-24. VII.2:1). Being is absolutely singular, not manifold. There are not several Beings. There is only one God. Beyond the differences of inner and outer, dark and light, good and bad, there is only Oneness. When it's cold, water freezes into ice; when it's warm, ice turn into water; when ego rules, mind freezes into form. Awakening, mind melts back into spirit. If the whole is likened to the ocean and the part likened to a drop of water, then when the drop becomes one with the ocean, it sees again with the eye of the ocean. Nothing is lost. Everything is gained.

*This fragment of your mind is such a tiny part of it that,*
*could you but appreciate the whole, you would see instantly*
*that it is like the smallest sunbeam to the sun,*
*or like the faintest ripple on the surface of the ocean.*
*In its amazing arrogance,*
*this tiny sunbeam has decided it is the sun;*
*this almost imperceptible ripple hails itself as the ocean.*

T-18.VIII.3:3–4

What happens when we love? We are lost, but we are found (Matthew 10:39). Losing ego means gaining the eternal. Losing an illusion is the acquisition of reality. How can a dream be real? How can an illusion be anything but an illusion; and, what do we lose when we lose an illusion? According to Austrian physicist Erwin Schrödinger (1887–1961), The overall number of minds is one. Division is uncertain by definition. It is in conflict because it is out of accord with itself. The ego, being separation itself, thinks of Oneness as something outside of itself. In Oneness, however, there is no place where God stops and you start. *Where God is, there are you. Such is the truth* (T-14.VIII.4:4–5).

> *You believe you can harbor thoughts you would not share,*
> *and that salvation lies in keeping thoughts to yourself alone.*
> *For in private thoughts, known only to yourself,*
> *you think you find a way to keep what you would have alone,*
> *and share what you would share. And then you wonder*
> *why it is that you are not in full communication*
> *with those around you,*
> *and with God Who surrounds all of you together.*

> T-15.IV.7:3–5

A study on happiness conducted by a group of social psychologists during the 1990s concluded that there is no one thing that can be said to make us happy. Happiness, they said, was subjective. Nevertheless, the study did find some basic traits of happiness. What made for happiness was nothing of the world: success, youth, good looks, money, or any of what are sometimes envied assets. The clear winner was close relationships. The study said that a supportive, intimate connection with others was the single most important ingredient in happiness. The thing which makes us the happiest is the experience of loving and being loved. The study concluded that the unhappiest people were obviously those who did not experience the give and take of a loving relationship. We literally are one. We are literally of one undivided Mind. Separation is unhappiness. Fortunately, we do not have to be with other bodies in order to experience

Oneness. The Course, thus, asks us, "Do you really think you are alone unless another body is with you" (W-76.3:4)? The Holy Spirit is always with us. As minds are joined, we are never alone. We cannot be separated from the Love of God.

Watch birds flying in synchronization or a school of fish all swimming as though guided by one mind. Each bird or fish is doing its own thing and yet they move as one. When the members of a symphony orchestra play together or dancers dance together, there is an inevitable exhilaration that comes with the profound sense of Oneness joined as One (T-25.I.7:1).

*Truth is so far beyond time that all of it happens at once.*
*For as it was created one, so its oneness depends not on time at all.*

T-15.II.1:9

## Omnipresence: The Whole in One

We might think of Oneness as omnipresence, or presence at all times and in all places. Dropping projection, we experience omnipresence and omnipresence brings compassion. Omnipresence is equanimity. In equanimity there is no division, no good and bad, attractive, and repulsive. Omnipresence is tranquility, ubiquitous, unbounded, everywhere, universal, and non-judgmental. Oneness is infinite mind. Oneness simply is. As Lesson 30 from the Course expresses it, "God is in everything I see *because* God is in my mind."

*Oneness is simply the idea God is. And in His Being,*
*He encompasses all things. No mind holds anything but Him.*
*We say, 'God is,' and then we cease to speak,*
*for in that knowledge words are meaningless*

W-169.5:1–4

*Oneness is endless, timeless, and within your grasp*
*because your hands are His.*

T-24.V.9:4

I went to dinner with a friend. We were seated in such a way that you could not help but hear the conversation at the table next to us. It was an older man and his wife. The man had experienced a revelation that day and he wanted to share it with his wife. He said, "You know what I realized today honey, we're all just people here." His wife, not being able to connect with what he was saying, asked him if they should paint or wallpaper the bathroom. He tried again, He said, "No, no, honey listen to me, you know, we're all just people here." And she said, "Should it be blue or yellow?" I realized then that he was sharing his insight with me so I could share it with you: "We're all just people here!"

# CHAPTER 17

# Above All Else

## STRENGTHENING MOTIVATION TO CHANGE

*All good teachers realize that only fundamental change*
*will last, but they do not begin at that level.*
*Strengthening motivation for change is their first*
*and foremost goal. It is also their last and final one.*
*Increasing motivation for change in the learner is*
*all that a teacher need do to guarantee change.*
**Change in motivation is a change of mind,**
*and this will inevitably produce fundamental change*
*because the mind is fundamental.*

T-6.V.B.2:1–5 (BOLD MINE)

A Hindu student approached his master while the master was standing in a river and told him that he wanted to be enlightened. The master reached out, grabbed the student by his neck, plunged his head under the water, and held it there for a couple of minutes. The student struggled mightily to get free. Finally, the master let go. When the student caught his breath and could talk again he said; "Why . . . why did you do that?" The master asked, "When you were under the water, what did you want more than anything else?" "More than anything," he said, "I wanted to be able to take a breath." "Then," the master said, "When you want to be enlightened as much as you want a breath of air, you can be enlightened." One of the things you love about the mystics is their profound love and devotion to God. God becomes the main desire of the heart. Ultimately, God is the only thing we want. So why should we not go for the ultimate? We don't go for the ultimate because we put our own dreaming of the world ahead of God.

> *Become in all things a God seeker*
> *and in all things a God finder*
> *at all times and in all places.*
>
> GERMAN MYSTIC MEISTER ECKHART (1260–1326)

The Holy Spirit is here to help us change our minds in a comfortable, non-judgmental atmosphere. To change, we must realize that:

1. There is a need for a change.
2. The mind can be changed; and,
3. There is a "better" way to see things.

> *The holy instant is the result of*
> *your determination to be holy. It is the answer.*
> *The desire and the willingness to let it come precedes its coming.*
> *You prepare your mind for it only to the extent of recognizing*
> *that you want it above all else.*
>
> T-18.IV.1:1–4

On May 7, 2001, I had a tumor the size of a lemon removed from my insides. The day after, I awoke to see the oncologist standing at the foot of my bed. His first words were, "Mr. Mundy, I have to tell you that the cancer has spread." It had gone into my lymph system. After that, I had to decide if I was going to follow a natural therapy program or was I going to go the way of chemotherapy. I asked Dr. Ken Wapnick his opinion and he said if I was to do the natural process, I should do it all the way. As with any spiritual discipline, to get results, it must be done all the way. As it turned out, I did both chemotherapy and a natural method started by a Dr. Richard Schultz, who also made it clear, "Either do this program or don't do it, but don't do it halfway." Eleven months later, I was cancer-free.

*You cannot be totally committed sometimes.*

T-7.VII.1:4

*Belief that there is another way of perceiving is the loftiest idea of which ego thinking is capable. That is because it contains a hint of recognition that the ego is not the Self.*

T-4.II.4:10

## Motivation and Need

A frog fell into a pothole and couldn't get out. Even his friends couldn't get him to muster enough strength to jump out of the deep pothole. Finally, they gave up and left him to his fate. The next day they saw him bounding around just fine. Somehow, he made it out. "How did you do it? We thought you couldn't get out." The frog replied, "I couldn't but a truck was coming and I had to."

A therapist friend tells the story of a client who was suing her company for discrimination and had developed panic attacks and a phobia of driving. When her dog got seriously ill and no one was around, she had to drive him to the vet. From that time on she was again able to drive. If we need food, or water, or we need to go to the bathroom, our motivation to fulfill our need is directly proportional to the level of our discomfort. When circumstances become unbearable, we are motivated to change. When love falls away from a marriage, when our health breaks down, when debt becomes unmanageable, we *might* change. We do not, however, need to wait for provocation to make a change. Procrastination is an avoidance of now.

## Reawakening Spiritual Vision

> *You can temporize and you are capable of enormous*
> *procrastination, but you cannot depart entirely from your Creator,*
> *Who set the limits on your ability to miscreate.*
>
> . . . . . . . . . .
>
> *Tolerance for pain may be high, but it is not without limit.*
> *Eventually everyone begins to recognize,*
> *however dimly, that there [must] be a better way.*
> *As this recognition becomes more firmly established,*
> *it becomes a turning point. This ultimately reawakens spiritual*
> *vision, simultaneously weakening the investment in physical sight.*

T-2.III.3:3 & 5–8

Whenever something tragic like cancer, a divorce, or bankruptcy happens, we can either change or regress into despair. We can always slip into denial, projection, dissociation, and addiction. Lesson number 20 from the Workbook is, "I am determined to see." Lesson number 21 is, "I am determined to see things differently." Lesson number 27 is, "Above all else I want to see things differently." To be free, I must want to be free *above all else*. I must be willing to do what is necessary to change. Do I really want the peace of God above all else? Or, do I still want to do things in my own way—on my own terms—in my own time—until time runs out?

If I have a headache, I take an aspirin and the pain goes away. Something from the outside changed things on the inside. Medicine treats the symptom but the cause has not changed. My headache is gone. The reason for the headache is not gone. If the mind has not changed, there has been no real change. All physical symptoms are caused by guilt in the mind. The guilty mind then projects a sick body. We can fix the symptom in the body. If, however, the guilt in the mind is not fixed, the same symptom or a new one will reappear.

A participant in a workshop on forgiveness suffered from migraine headaches. They started, she said, when she was in a relationship which ended badly. She was continually angry and unforgiving. She realized during the workshop that she did not have any choice. She was *going to have to forgive herself* and the man in question. She decided to be free of the whole mess—to let it all go. She decided that what had happened didn't make any difference; that she actually didn't need to do anything except to let go of her hatred for the man in question. Later she reported that to her surprise, the headaches had not returned and having let it all go, she now felt marvelously free.

There is a Buddhist story about two monks who were walking from one village to another and they had to ford a river. There was a young woman standing on the bank of the river who wanted to cross to the other side. One monk offered to take her to the other side by letting her ride on his back as he waded across. He put her down on the other side and the two monks continued on their journey. The other monk began burning up inside slowly, becoming increasingly incensed, as Buddhist monks were not to touch women. After a couple of hours of silence he said to his companion, "How could you have let that woman touch you?" To which the other monk responded, "I left her back by the river. You are still carrying her."

*Learning and wanting to learn are inseparable.*
*You learn best when you believe*
*what you are trying to learn is of value to you.*

T-4.V.3:5–6

If I am studying Spanish because I know that I am going to spend time in Spain, I am more motivated to actually learn Spanish than I will be if I do not plan on someday using the language. If I am going to play a piano for a recital, my motivation to learn to play a particular piece of music is obviously increased. In order to learn what the Course has to teach, I have to actually do what it is asking me to do.

*You want to be happy. You want peace.*
*You do not have them now,*
**because your mind is totally undisciplined,**
*and you cannot distinguish between*
*joy and sorrow, pleasure and pain, love and fear.*
*You are now learning how to tell them apart.*
*And great indeed will be your reward.*

W-20.2:3–8 (BOLD MINE)

## Discipline and the Mind

The word discipline comes from the word *disciple*. A disciple is a follower of a teacher or a teaching. The teacher brings a teaching. Jesus is a Rabbi—a teacher. Our minds are *totally* undisciplined. Being undisciplined, we have work to do before we can be healed and whole. We have to purify our perception to remove fear. How much time is given to compulsions, to hungers of the body we "seem" unable to control? And, who is the "we" who cannot control it? When we dissociate, get caught in a projection, or side-tracked by some habituated activity, we do not even attempt to try to control our minds. An addict does not attempt to control a craving. The addiction has won.

> *There is no need to learn through pain.*
> *And gentle lessons are acquired joyously,*
> *and are remembered gladly.*
> *What gives you happiness you want to learn and not forget.*

> T-21.I.3:1–3

Epictetus, the ancient Greek Stoic philosopher, said peace comes from living a simple life in which we learn to control the mind and to trim away both *aversions* and *desires*. Aversions are things we project against. We are called upon to be free of *all* denials and projections. Aversions are things we can't stand and try to stay away from. Desires are things we try to get more of. Wanting something or wanting to push something away from us, makes the thing real. When we fall in love, we desire that person more than anything. Then, when we get divorced, we try to push that person out of our lives.

My friend, Lori Coburn, tells the story of a young man who fell in love with a girl who had this "cute little gap" between her front teeth. Later, when they broke up, she became "that gap-toothed bitch." Both extreme behaviors, both judgments, first good then bad, both reinforce the idea that something or someone exterior to us can make us happy or unhappy.

> *Just as polishing iron can turn it into a mirror so can*
> *a mind conditioned by discipline eliminates its mental rust.*

> SUFI MYSTIC GHAZZALI (1058–1111)

To let go of the pollutants, the blocks to the awareness of love's presence, *the stuff* that is getting in the way of spiritual progress, calls for vigilance and correction with Spirit. This is not hard work. In fact, it is much easier than not working. Not working (unconsciousness and dissociation) leads to despair and depression. We will eventually awaken, so why not awaken now?

> *When you have learned how to decide with God,*
> *all decisions become as easy and as right as breathing.*
> *There is no effort, and you will be led as gently as if*
> *you were being carried down a quiet path in summer.*
> *Only your own volition seems to make deciding hard.*
>
> T-14.IV.6:1–3

## Mind-Wandering and Mind-Training

We can probably all think of times when Spirit urged us to go one way; we went another and later wished we had not. If something goes "against our better judgment," it's a good idea to stop, look, listen, and ask for correction. We are much too tolerant of *mind-wandering*. We may call it meditation but mind-wandering is often simply dissociation, self-indulgence, rehearsal of the past, and day-dreaming. Mind-wandering *is* projection. It takes us away from rather than toward Oneness. It can be recognized and corrected. A split or dissociated mind does not know what it wants. A unified and disciplined mind rests in contentment. With a unified mind, we simply go ahead and do what we are being asked to do. The real question is not why can't I hear the voice of the Holy Spirit, the real question is why don't I do what He is asking me to do so I can hear his voice even better?

> *You have seen the extent of your lack of mental discipline,*
> *and of your need for mind training. It is necessary that you be*
> *aware of this, for it is indeed a hindrance to your advance.*
>
> W-95.4:4

"Ah, but," you say, "I don't want to be brainwashed." We're already brainwashed and 99.9 percent of the time, we listen to the indoctrination that comes from the ego and a consensus reality created and sustained by television, magazines, the radio, the internet, our neighbors, and more. Our minds are very undisciplined, very untrained. Our ability to listen to the Holy Spirit depends on our willingness to question our wandering minds, our machinations, fearful fantasies, beliefs, and illusions.

*. . . when the mind is occupied with a name or form*
*it will grasp that alone. When the mind expands*
*in the form of countless thoughts, each thought becomes weak;*
*but as thoughts get resolved the mind becomes one-pointed and strong,*
*for such a mind Self-inquiry will become easy.*

INDIAN SAGE RAMANA MAHARSHI (1879–1950),

IN *THE SPIRITUAL TEACHING OF RAMANA MAHARSHI*

## Clarity and Commitment

Trying to give part of my commitment to God and part to the ego, I wind up with no definite results. A definite result is the experience of peace of mind. The more I pay attention to the Holy Spirit, the more I can't help doing what God would have me do. True discipline is remembering what we really want. Being disciplined, the positive result is automatic. The right hand does not have to let the left hand know what to do. The pianist does not think about where to place his fingers on the piano keys. The awakened mind does not "think" about the appropriate response.

*Say to the Holy Spirit only, "Decide for me," and it is done.*
*For His decisions are reflections of what God knows about you,*
*and in this light, error of any kind becomes impossible.*
*Why would you struggle so frantically to anticipate*
*all you cannot know, when all knowledge lies behind*
*every decision the Holy Spirit makes for you?*

T-14.III.16.1:1–3

# CHAPTER 18

───────

# A Course in Mind Training

## CHANGING OUR MINDS—CHANGING OUR LIVES

*This is a course in mind training.*
*All learning involves attention and study at some level.*

T-1.4:1

*You have seen the extent of your lack of mental discipline,*
*and of your need for mind training.*
*It is necessary that you be aware of this,*
*for it is indeed a hindrance to your advance.*

W-95.4:4

*Learning through rewards is more effective*
*than learning through pain,*
*because pain is an ego illusion,*
*and can never induce more than a temporary effect.*

T-4.VI.3:4

## We're All Addictive

We easily develop special relationships with food, drink, drugs, sex, money, and each other. We are addicted to our attitudes, prejudicial thoughts, traditions, customs, mores, and more. We are addicted to our "mind-set," to our ways of seeing and being in the world. Habits and addictions often run our lives with little or no awareness on our own part. We do things regularly, ritually—routinely. The word "addiction" comes from the Latin *addictus* meaning something we *yield* to, something we are *devoted* to, something that we *crave*. The daily, repetitive use of any habitual activity can *hurt* or *help, retard*, or *facilitate* our physical, mental, and spiritual being. To allow mistakes to continue is to make additional mistakes. Recognizing and correcting destructive patterns of thinking and adopting constructive ones can facilitate our well-being; in fact, the healthy use of thoughtful patterns is a way of collapsing time rather than the continuance of time through dreaming (T-1.II.6:9). For this reason the workbook lessons in the Course are designed to help us to think more creatively and more peacefully.

> *I have enjoined you to behave as I behaved,*
> *but we must respond to the same Mind to do this.*
> *This Mind is the Holy Spirit, Whose Will is for God always.*
> *He teaches you how to keep me as the model for your thought,*
> *and to behave like me as a result.*
>
> T-5.II.12:1–3

## Why Do We Do What We Do?

We may think our mother's cooking is (or was) the best, not because it is (or was) the best. We think it the best because we kept putting her food in our mouths, day in and day out, year in and year out. If I keep putting a certain kind of food in my mouth I'll soon begin to crave it.

*You cannot separate yourself from the truth*
*by "giving" autonomy to behavior.*

T-2.VI.2:8

Our thinking patterns are as ingrained in us as the accent that characterizes the sound of our speech. If you grow up in England, Boston, Argentina, or Russia you have a distinct accent. Actors sometimes have to change their accents to play certain roles. So, too, can we, with the same simplicity, change our minds if we are willing to try it. It takes, however, a little willingness. Changing the mind then means being involved in a "process" of change. Animals live with inherent dispositions toward specific behaviors. They build nests, raise their young, grow old, and die without the neurosis and psychosis which characterizes the human mind. Interestingly, the only animals which develop neurosis are those we place in cages or those who live in our homes according to our rules. "No, no, bad dog!"

We develop an identity based on our fundamental predispositions, and inherited customs. We live not by reason; we live rather on impulse, convention, and routine reactions. We buy the game; we play the game, and the more we play the game, the more the game plays us. The more we lose sight of the game, the more we think the game is real—the less we can remember God.

Eventually, everything returns to God. It is headed that way. It always has been. Though a thousand paths present themselves, they are all detours and distractions, save—to follow the Voice for God. In order to get "Home," I have to give up *all* the ego's many distractions so I might as well start cleaning house now so I can be happy now.

*Only the self-accused condemn.*

*As you prepare to make a choice that will result in different outcomes, there is first one thing that must be overlearned. It must become a habit of response so typical of everything you do that it becomes your first response to all temptation, and to every situation that occurs.*

*Learn this, and learn it well, for it is here delay of happiness is shortened by a span of time you cannot realize.*

*You never hate your brother for his sins, but only for your own.*

*Whatever form his sins appear to take, it but obscures the fact that you believe them to be yours, and therefore meriting a "just" attack.*

T-31.III.1:1–6

We resist being like our mothers and fathers only to notice as we get older that we are very much like them. How aware are any of us of the programming that came from our family, neighbors, school, the church, and the greater society in which we live, the country of which we are a part. More than anything in the twenty-first century—television is telling us its vision.

## Changing Our Minds—Changing Our Lives

According to the Greek philosopher Aristotle (384 BCE–322 BCE), moral excellence or virtue comes about via habit. "We are what we do," said Aristotle. Excellence is a habit we cultivate. A good habit enables us to make right decisions. "Virtue," said Aristotle "is a set of skills gradually developed over time through practice." We condition ourselves through patterns of thinking, which is why "it makes no small difference whether we form habits of one kind or another from our very youth" (from *The Nichomachean Ethics*). Our thoughts become "second nature" and an integral part of character.

> *Routines as such are dangerous,*
> *because they easily become gods in their own right,*
> *threatening the very goals for which they were set up.*

M-16.2:5

American philosopher William James (1842–1910) was fascinated with the study of habituated patterns of thinking and with mysticism. According to James, "habit is second nature, or rather, ten time's nature." G.I. Gurdjieff (1866–1949), the Greek-Armenian mystic and spiritual teacher, said that most people sleepwalk through life. Our true identity can, thus, only be known when we recognize and ask for correction for routines. "Only reason," says Gurdjieff, "can change being."

> *You do not realize the whole extent to which the idea of separation*
> *has interfered with reason.*
> *Reason lies in the other self you have cut off from your awareness.*
> *And nothing you have allowed to stay in your awareness is capable*
> *of reason. How can the segment of the mind devoid of reason*
> *understand what reason is, or grasp the information it would give?*

T-21.V.4:1–3

Aristotle, Nietzsche, James, and Gurdjieff saw dispositions, habits, and instincts, as integral to the development of a spiritual life. For each, morality is a continuous chain of actions which arise out of inner nature. Therefore, the thoughts we develop are of paramount importance.

The Course is trying to get us back to that which is natural and reasonable. It is trying to help us regain possession of our minds so we can give our "minds" back to The Mind. We are moving from mindlessness to

Mindfulness. This is a world of mindlessness. We have literally forgotten who we are. We think we are bodies trapped in a world, in space and time. To return to Mindfulness, to return to that which is natural, I have to be willing to take a step beyond the confined habituate process of thinking adopted in the dreaming of the world. Realizing the power of the mind and how much we have overlearned the ego's lessons and how easily we become addicted to wrong-minded thinking, psychologist William Glasser, PhD, wrote a best-selling book titled, *Positive Addiction* in 1976. Seeing how we are so easily addicted, he suggested that we try to develop some habits which help rather than hinder our progress through life.

*Positive addiction is something anyone can try for.*
*There is no risk. Since all positive addictions are simple activities*
*that can be easily accomplished, there is no possibility of failure in*
*what you attempt to do. What is hard is to do them long enough to*
*become addicted, but if you quit you are no worse off.*

AMERICAN PSYCHIATRIST WILLIAM GLASSER (1925–PRESENT)

## Characteristics of Negative Habits

As we go through this first list, think of any debilitating habit, like compulsive overeating, drinking, smoking, gambling, shopping, etc., notice how many addictions are related to so-called bodily appetites, which are according to the Course not physical in origin. Anything a body does must first be a thought.

1.  **We choose to do it.** We devote time to it. One good test for a "true" addiction is, that it is probably something we do everyday. An alcoholic drinks every day.

2. **We do it easily.** It does not take a great deal of effort to light a cigarette, pour another drink, or "veg out" in front of the television.

3. **We often do it alone.** As we are not proud of ourselves when we engage a negative addiction, we often hide the fact that we do it.

4. **It *seems* to have value for us.** Smoking may calm us down, drinking may help us (temporarily) forget our problems, a drug may help us to "space out."

5. **We criticize ourselves when we do it.** We know that it is hurtful to us and yet that fact does not stop us.

6. **If we persist at it, things will get worse,** our health will deteriorate, and our relationship will suffer. We will be less effective in our work, our finances will be depleted, and our self-esteem destroyed.

## Characteristics of Positive Habits

The first three characteristics are the same as for a negative thought pattern. The fourth, fifth, and sixth are similar and yet completely different.

1. **We choose to do it.** We devote time to it. We may or may not do it every day.

2. **We do it easily.** It does not take a great deal of effort to do it. According to Aristotle, moral action is easier and more pleasurable than immoral action. It is *effortless* to be nice. It requires energy to be unpleasant.

3. **We can do it alone.** It is non-competitive—walking, reading, writing, playing a musical instrument and meditation are examples of positive, "solo" acts and patterns.

4. **It has value for us.** It enriches and improves our life mentally, physically, financially, socially (emotionally), and/or spiritually.

5. **We do not criticize ourselves when we do it.** In fact, we feel better when we do it.

6. **If we persist at it, things will get better.** Our health, finances, and relationships will improve. If we persist long enough, we might master our art and become a specialist, expert, a virtuoso in our field.

## Creating New Patterns: Asking for Spirit's Guidance

*The habit of engaging with God and His creations is easily made
if you actively refuse to let your mind slip away.*

T-4.IV.7:1

S top reading and lace your fingers together. Look at which thumb is on top. We habitually do it the same way without thinking. Now redo it, and this time, *consciously* switch the thumbs. Doing so "nudges" us into a slightly different neurological pathway. Do anything repeatedly, and before long it will become automatic. We *do not think* about where our fingers go when we type on a computer. Pianists *do not think* about where to place their fingers on the piano. To switch our thumbs, we have to "think" first. We do not think about following the ego, we do not plan on being judgmental and projective. It is so ingrained, we do it automatically. We literally, "do not think" about what we are doing. To switch thinking from the ego to the Holy Spirit, "think" first. Look at the judgment. See it and then laugh at it, smile at it, and then let it go. It takes a little willingness and yet before long, following inner guidance and developing miracle-mindedness can, with time, become as natural as breathing because it is the most natural thing of all.

*Miracles are habits, and should be involuntary.*
*They should not be under conscious control.*

PRINCIPLE NUMBER 5 OF THE 50 MIRACLES PRINCIPLES T-1.1:5

It takes consistent effort to retrain the mind. I've read four suggestions as to how long it takes to make or break an addiction, twenty-one days, thirty days, forty days, and "just about forever." With consistent effort, we may *either discontinue* or develop a new pattern of thinking, and thus, a new way of being. When breaking a physical addiction, like alcohol, smoking, or drugs, we must *persevere*—to become free. Jesus, in Luke 11:18, speaks of the importance of importunity (consistent asking). We should not be surprised that when it comes to breaking our addiction to the ego, it's going to require persistence. Indeed the ego will resist mightily. As the ego was not developed in a day, it takes willingness to change our thinking patterns and yet:

*Where all reality has been withdrawn from what was never true,*
*can it be hard to give it up, and choose what must be true?*

T-26.III.7:7

*Miracles represent freedom from fear.*
*"Atoning" means "undoing." The undoing of fear*
*is an essential part of the Atonement value of miracles.*

PRINCIPLE NUMBER 26 OF THE 50 MIRACLES PRINCIPLES T-1.1.26

## Undoing, Purification, and Purging

Alcoholics Anonymous, the most successful program for dealing with alcoholism, is a process of deprogramming or undoing. The principles of Alcoholics Anonymous, according to Dr. Bob, one of the co-founders of Alcoholics Anonymous, can be expressed in six words: *Trust God. Clean house. Help others.* When someone in an Alcoholics Anonymous recovery program encounters distress they can call a sponsor and/or attend a meeting. When distress is encountered while studying the Course, call on the Holy Spirit for help. The Holy Spirit is available 24/7 and you will never get a busy signal or have to leave a message. Just get quiet and move to a place of "reasonableness" (sanity) within the mind.

> *Give up what you do not want, and keep what you do.*
> *How simple is the obvious!*
>
> M-4.I.A.6:6

Happiness comes in finding freedom from the ego. Purification in the physical sense is traditionally understood as the burning off of the slough, the rust, the unnecessary debt, the extra weight, the burdening judgments, and ego demands placed on the world and on us. In the same way, in forgiving, we let go of what is not true and release our projections so that truth can move to the fore. Mystics often describe a series of steps or stages in the development of a mystical life. Mystics, with as widely different backgrounds as Evelyn Underhill, Theresa of Avila, Sufism, Bernadette Roberts, and Gurdjieff all describe as the first step in spiritual development is *purgation*. Purgation means purifying, getting rid of the unessential, cleansing, clarifying, etc.

> *The first step toward freedom*
> *involves a sorting out of the false from the true.*
>
> T-2.VIII.4:1

I do some counseling by phone. Very often when someone calls, it will be because of some "issue" they have, usually having something to do with someone else and the way they have been treated, offended by, or disappointed by a boyfriend, girlfriend, husband, wife, employer, etc. It usually takes about twenty minutes for them to "spit it out" or "regurgitate" the "poison" that has built up inside. Then when they finally settle down, I've noticed that my most usual response is to say, "You know I think you're going to have to let this go." And though I may not say it, I think, "Because this is making you sick."

My friend, Jeannine Caryl, described her experience in stopping smoking. She was proselytizing to a young man about the power of God and at the same time, she was smoking a cigarette. She said to the young man, "God can do anything." To which the young man replied. "If God can do anything, then why can't God help you stop smoking?" The next day, as she lit a cigarette, she remembered the incident with the young man from the previous day. She snuffed out the cigarette and never smoked again. It was a simple matter of a decision. We can be seduced by the ego (our seeming needs and wants) or we can choose to see it God's way. Letting go of the ego isn't easy but it becomes progressively easier as we turn it over to Holy Spirit. Correction belongs at the level where change is possible. We need guidance at the mind level (T-2.IV.5:3–4). If the mind changes everything changes.

## The Holiness Habit

Every single moment of every single day, we are at choice. We are always at a point of "decision," between truth and illusion. Doing God's will, which is our own Will, is freedom. This makes no sense to the ego. To the ego, if God wins, we lose. Truth is—it is only as God wins that we win. We can be free or we can remain a slave. We *know* when we are choosing for the ego and we *know* when we choose for God. Right-mindedness is the "will" to turn it over.

> *You must change your mind, not your behavior,*
> *and this is a matter of willingness.*
> *You do not need guidance except at the mind level.*
> *Correction belongs only at the level where change is possible.*

T-2.VI.3:4–6

Awakening means choosing the right mind and thus, ceasing to give control to the ego. Awakening, mind melts into spirit. It is a matter of choice. Resisting temptation is a matter of will—not "will power," just willingness. It is simply a choice to see correctly. There is no need to attack or "dethrone" the ego. I simply cease giving power to it.

> *Your practice must therefore rest*
> *upon your willingness to let all littleness go.*

T-15.IV.2:1

Each fall and spring, when it is cleanup time in our community, the Department of Sanitation trucks come around and picks up old rugs, broken appliances, furniture, etc. One thing you notice are a number of "ab loungers" and "tummy trainers," out along the curb. It was a good idea maybe but obviously it is not something which is being used. Despite the presence of these gadgets, the fact remains—the best way to lose weight is not to eat too much; and, if I want to work on my abs, I can go for a walk, do crunches, sit-ups, leg lifts, and more. There is no need for special equipment. No pills or magical formula is required. What is required is not magic. It is simply a choice. Who is the decider? In a similar way, spiritual development requires discipline, and regular daily, hourly, sometimes minute-by-minute commitment to the truth. In other words, it means practice.

> *Structure, then, is necessary for you at this time,*
> *planned to include frequent reminders of your goal*
> *and regular attempts to reach it. Regularity . . . is advantageous,*
> *for those whose motivation is inconsistent,*
> *and who remain heavily defended against learning.*
>
> W-95.6:1–3

The workbook of the Course is here to help us with our daily practice and the better we get in our practice the greater the ease with which we come to live the Course. There is no set way to do the lessons in the Workbook, though it's best to begin and end the day doing a lesson. Some folks write the lesson on a post-it notepad and then put it someplace where it can be seen throughout the day—on the side of the computer screen, in the checkbook, or on the dash of the car. Some folks leave a copy of the Course in the bathroom where they can sit reading over a lesson at the beginning of each day. Read the lesson before stepping into the shower and then repeat the lesson while in the shower. Make it a screen-saver on the computer. The methodology is less important than our willingness to remember to do what is asked of us.

> *Forgiveness is acquired.*
> *It is not inherent in the mind, which cannot sin.*
> *As sin is an idea you taught yourself,*
> *forgiveness must be learned by you*
> *as well, but from a Teacher other than yourself,*
> *Who represents the other*
> *Self in you. Through Him you learn how to forgive the self you think*
> *you made, and let it disappear.*

*Thus you return your mind as one to Him*
*Who is your Self, and Who can never sin.*

W-121.6:1–5

Miracles are habits and forgiveness can become a habit. Patience can become a habit. Kindness can become a habit. We develop forgiveness by doing it repeatedly. So much so that it becomes an automatic. When it becomes an automatic we do not have to think about what our response is going to do, we just do it "naturally." In fact, after a while, I don't have to do it. That is, I don't have to think about doing it any more than a truly reformed alcoholic has to think about not drinking.

*The lessons you have taught yourself have been so*
*overlearned and fixed they rise like heavy curtains to obscure*
*the simple and the obvious.*

T-31.I.3:4

## Over-Learning

There is a theory in education called over-learning. Repeat any activity over and over again and it will be encoded in the brain. Most everyone has over-learned how to tie their shoes. Men over-learn how to tie ties. When studying a foreign language, we learn a new word; but then we review it again and again. In this way, it is less likely that we will forget it. In the same way with music, I practice a piece until I know it; and then, I practice it again. We have so over-learned the lessons of the ego that it should not surprise us to hear that it's going to take some discipline to learn a wholly new habit. Though we "know" that projection makes perception, we've been engaging in the process of judgment so much we must repeatedly catch ourselves and stop it, catch ourselves and stop it, catch ourselves and stop it, up to the point where we no longer have to catch ourselves—we just don't go there.

Though there is no requirement to do so, some students of the Course, once they complete the Workbook, do it over again. Reading the text again, the text becomes increasingly clear because we are now able to hear it at a yet deeper level. Likewise, over-learning means we don't forget. As we begin to live the Course, as we get better at it, we literally develop the habit of miracle-mindedness.

# CHAPTER 19

# Word Fasting: The Spiritual Diet

## OBSERVING AND CORRECTING OUR THOUGHTS

*And so we start our journey beyond words*
*by concentrating first on what impedes your progress still.*

W-PI.IN.181–200.3:1

## Let's Review Briefly

Projection makes perception. Understanding this three-word sentence is crucial in our understanding the Course. I project the world as "real" not "realizing" that I am an image maker. I dream a dream. Every word is a projection within the dream. Everything changes when we change the way we see. First, I must remember that I have a mind which can be changed. A miracle is a change of mind from mindlessness, misthought, wrong-mindedness, or insanity to mindfulness, right-mindedness, sanity, or "reasonableness." The body *acts* wrongly only when it responds to *misthought*. We are trying to regain control of our minds, and thus, our misthoughts, so that being free of misthoughts, we can learn to think again (bring our minds back) in line with the Mind of God. God is Love. God is Life. Life is Thought. God is Mind. We are part of God (T-5.II.5:5). God's Voice speaks to us all through the day (W-49).

*The body can act wrongly only when it is responding to misthought.*

T-2.IV.2:5

Our minds are composed of bits of information called words. While words are "symbols of symbols," they remain (along with sensations, feelings, and intuitions) a primary instrument in our learning. The Course is written in words. You are reading words which convey ideas that can help us "change our minds."

*Would you know how many times you merely thought*
*you were right, without ever realizing you were wrong?*

M-10.4:4

There is something in us which loves techniques and the following are techniques, *practical suggestions*—a means of observing our thoughts and correcting them by becoming progressively more aware of language, and thus, the misthought which produces the language. Everyone likes to be right and the ego is more concerned with *control* than it is with *sanity*. The ego, however, keeps this motivation from our awareness. The following suggested exercise is simply a way of recognizing that what we say is an outward reflection of an inner condition which needs correction. Just as anger is a sure sign that our thinking is *off course* and we need a better way of seeing; so too, becoming more aware of our language helps us see where and how we get stuck within an ego framework. From this vantage point, we might then choose once again. Remember, "every choice you make establishes your own identity as you will see it and believe it is" (T-31.VIII.6:6).

Sigmund Freud pointed out the importance of slips of tongue and jokes which say a great deal about our own unconscious. In like manner, we'll be looking at the following words in order to be more conscious of our own thinking patterns so we might thereby see where we get stuck in ego thinking. We might then become more conscious of what we are doing and redirect our thinking away from the "guidance" of the ego. We think our judgments make us right. They are, however, *just* judgments. As each thought arises, observe: to whom does this thought occur? We are learning to question the value of the ego as a guide in life.

*Watch your mind carefully for any beliefs that hinder its accomplishment, and step away from them.*

T-4.IV.8:5

This *technique,* if employed, can enable a growing awareness of the level of insanity we have adopted. Through this process, we can see what "pushes our buttons." What do we do when we go on a diet? We cut out certain foods, or we cut back on the amount of food or both. To go on a monetary diet, we cut back on spending. Problems arise when we overdo, when we overspend, overeat, drink too much, or "overplay" the severity of a situation. The solution is to cut back, to cut out; to drop projective thinking—to say nothing. One simple way to observe projections is to watch the words that come out of our mouth. We can, thus, "let go" of the kind of thinking which keeps us from happiness. We cannot, however, change our thinking, if we do not know that it is misguided.

*Sometimes a sin can be repeated over and over, with obviously distressing results, but without the loss of its appeal.*
*And suddenly, you change its status from a sin to a mistake.*
*Now you will not repeat it; you will merely stop and let it go, unless the guilt remains.*

T-19.III.3:3—5

We set aside the old in order for the new to come to the fore. The snake sheds its skin so that a new skin can emerge from below. Our bodies dispel old cells to make way for new ones. In a similar way, having built up a number of defenses against the truth, we should not be surprised to find that, as we become progressively miracle-minded, there is a setting aside of old habits and thoughts which no longer serve us. Alcohol makes certain folks obstinate, headstrong, and argumentative. Former alcoholics and drug addicts say that even within a few days after they stop drinking, they begin to experience increasing clarity of thought. They even find themselves *wanting* to be nice to others. As a member of AA once expressed it to me, "It's nice to wake up in the morning instead of 'coming to' in the morning."

> *The more you approach the center of His thought system,*
> *the clearer the light becomes.*
>
> T-11.IN.3:4

Just as "disease" is a sign that something is wrong with the body, so is our distemper (the upsetting of a natural balance), a sign of a certain "pollution" or "disease" of the mind. We need, therefore, a mind-cleaning. If we do not wash out the stone and the sand, how can we find the gold? Just as dropping smoking, drinking, or drugs means we've begun to purify our body, so dropping certain words from our language can be a valuable guide in helping us to clarify our thinking. It also helps us identify when we are having thoughts that need correction.

> *I have often repented of having spoken.*
> *I have never repented of not having spoken.*
>
> GERMAN MYSTIC HENRY SUESE (1295–1366)

## Every Word Is a Projection

According to "You Are What You Say," by Jan Donges, in the July/August 2009 issue of *Scientific American Mind* Magazine, a wealth of psychological insights can be gained by looking at the words that come out of our mouth—even the use of "little" words like pronouns. The frequency with which we use the word "I," for example, says a great deal about us. Every word is a statement, a declaration, an announcement, a proclamation, an assertion coming out of the void—made in the world. The first cry of a baby coming out of the womb is a projection—a statement. The baby was so very warm and well-nourished in the womb and now there are bright lights and sounds, and someone grabbing a hold of it. With words, we label, concretize, solidify, and make real. What is the first job given to Adam? He has to name things (Genesis 2:20). He begins by naming the animals. What is the first thing we learn in pre-school? We learn "words." What is the first thing we do in a high-school biology class? We begin by *labeling* the names of the parts of a flower or a frog.

*This universe, superimposed upon God, is nothing but a name.*

INDIAN VEDANTIST SHANKARA (788(?)–820(?))

Naming creates duality. It distinguishes the things that are named from the things that are unnamed. Miracle-mindedness hears only one voice—"the inner voice of reason (love)." The inner voice of reason is, however, easily drowned out by the ego's voice of outrage. The words that come out of our mouths are obvious expressions of our inner thoughts and personalities.

## Word Fasting

*God offers only mercy. Your words should reflect only mercy,*
*because that is what you have received*
*and that is what you should give.*

T-3.VI.6:1–2

Jesus, in the Gospels, says it is not what we put in our mouths that defile us; it's what comes out of the mouth that defiles us (Mark 7:15). A "word fast" is one way to catch the tricky ego at play. We may then avoid falling into its clutches. Looking at the words which come out of our mouths is a good way to begin to become aware of the extent of our own shadows.

1.  **Watch for Profanity and Vulgarities**
    While watching a "reality" television show specifically designed for teenagers with Sarah, my then-teenage daughter, we soon noticed that the language of the participants had to be frequently "bleeped." To damn a thing to hell is obviously a projection. I once took a friend to church with me. After the Sunday morning message we had a discussion. During the discussion, she kept talking about things which "pissed her off." Why would we say, "Shit?" Why would I ever want to refer to someone else as an asshole? One day in the cafeteria at the college where I used to teach, I could not help but overhear the conversation among a group of students at the next table. They had but one "f***ing" adjective for everything they evaluated as good or bad.

2.  **Watch for Name Calling**
    We may try to correct others by telling them off and making them feel guilty, thinking this will make them

change. This process, rather than providing a cure, creates a sense of separation between ourselves and others and it increases our sense of guilt. Our focus is on clearing up our own "mistakes," not projecting onto others. As we do, we begin to affect the other in a very subtle non-verbal way. It is helpful, therefore, to notice the use of name calling words like *stupid, insane, ludicrous, ridiculous, idiotic,* and *absurd.* These words are all highly projective and condemnatory. We would not want these words used in reference to ourselves, why would we want to use them in reference to another who (though perhaps wearing a disguise) is still one of our brothers; and therefore, one with us?

> *Would you condemn your brothers or free them?*

T-11.2:2

3. **Watch for "Dis" Word**

During the years when I taught in Sing Sing prison, I noticed that one of the worse things a prisoner could have happen to him was to have another prisoner or guard "Dis" him—to disrespect him. "Hey, he dissed me, man." Everybody needs respect. "Dis" comes from the Latin word *dis,* meaning "to render apart" or "asunder." We can only be *dis-appointed* if we have an appointment; an expectation or anticipation about the way a situation is supposed to look. If it doesn't look that way—we get to be disappointed. A friend once gave me a little plaque with the innocent face of a cocker spaniel puppy on it and under the picture was the caption. "Blessed are those who expect nothing for they will not be disappointed." Only an ego can be *disappointed.* To tell a child that we are disappointed in them is to place a burden on them. Children need our encouragement not our condemnation.

- To be *dis-eased* we must first have been at ease.
- We can only be *dis-illusioned* if we are living with an illusion.
- We can only be *dis-enchanted* if we are first *enchanted*.

4. **Watch for "Counting on"**

I once gave a talk at a conference. It was one of those times when everything seemed to flow very well. I was told by the producers that it was being taped (which it was), and I would be given a copy. There were lots of unplanned good laughs during the talk and I was looking forward to having a new recording. I waited for a couple of weeks and, not having received the CD, I called and was told that the recording did not work. I saw the response I was about to give before it came out—knowing it was coming from ego—"Oh, that's too bad. I was counting on that." Only an ego counts on things. Only an ego places expectations and anticipations on the world.

5. **Watch for "Disgusted," "Irked," and "Vulgar"**

*Watch your mind for the temptations of the ego,*
*and do not be deceived by it. It offers you nothing.*

T-4.IV.6:1–2

Watch for heavily judgmental words. Consider the word disgusted. It is a highly judgmental word. Who are we to be "disgusted"? On another occasion, a friend kept saying, "It irks the hell out of me." Disgusted, vulgar, and irked represent something which comes up from the gut; something which makes us sick. The choice to condemn takes our peace of mind away from us. Did you ever think that someone was "rude" or "uncouth"? Are things "appalling," "horrendous," "inexcusable," or "atrocious"? Is it really, or is our judgment about a thing keeping us from seeing? To take offense is to give offense.

6. **Watch for "Despicable"**

"Despicable" comes from *de* meaning "down" and *specere* "to look on," as in *denigrate*. Alexander Hamilton, the first Secretary of the Treasury of the United States, and the then vice-president of the United States Aaron Burr, were longtime political rivals. In 1804, Hamilton was quoted in the Albany Register saying that he thought something Burr had done was "despicable." Burr demanded an apology and when it was not forthcoming, Burr challenged Hamilton to a duel. They dueled in Weehawken, New Jersey, and Aaron Burr killed Alexander Hamilton over the word "despicable." I once heard an American historian say that he thought that of all the founding fathers, the one with the highest IQ was Alexander Hamilton. He devised the banking system that we use to this day. He had sixty people working in his department when others had only five. He may have had a high IQ, but it seems a low EQ (Emotional Quotient).

*. . . just a word, a little whisper that you do not like,*
*a circumstance that suits you not, or an event that*
*you did not anticipate upsets your world, and hurls it into chaos.*
*Truth is not frail.*
*Illusions leave it perfectly unmoved and undisturbed.*
*But specialness is not the truth in you.*
*It can be thrown off balance by anything.*

T-24.III.3:1–5

7. **Watch for "Upset" or "Offended"**

"Upset" and "offended" are indications of the loss of balance. To be upset, we must first have a *set-up*. We set it up, so we could be upset. The English word "upset" comes from the German *aufsetzen* meaning to overturn or capsize as we might lose our balance in a canoe. One translation for "upset" in Spanish is *trastornado* meaning to have a tornado, or twister. If we're upset, we're like Joe Btfsplk, the cartoon character from the Li'l Abner cartoon series who always walked around with a thunderstorm over the top of its head. If I can be hurt by anyone, then I am saying that that someone else is a sinner and that person has power over me—they have the power to take away my peace of mind. In a place of inner balance, we cannot be upset. In a similar way, if we are *off-ended*, something pushes us "off the end." Only an ego can be offended.

8. **Watch for Being Outraged or Insulted**

"Outrage" comes from the Anglo-French *ut-rage*, or *outer* or *uter*—like *other*. It's the *other* that's the problem. Outrage means we are "raging out." The word outraged is frequently used on the evening news as in—"The community is outraged by recent development at the local school." To be "outraged," we must feel that either we or others have been injured or insulted. "Insult" comes from the Latin *insultar*, meaning to leap upon or assail. Could Jesus be insulted? If we think we have been wronged or insulted, it's a good time to stop, look, and listen. We cannot be insulted unless we think we can. Could any enlightened being be insulted? Does what I see make me outraged? Is there ever a time when we could be justifiably outraged? No, Nunca,

Never! Anyone can say all manner of evil against us and it will have no effect on us, if we know who we are in truth.

*Teach no one he has hurt you, for if you do,*
*you teach yourself that what is not of God has power over you.*

T-14.III.8:2

### 9. Watch for "Bugged"

Sometimes just a little word shows how we give our peace away. I was talking with an amazing man, a physics professor who loved to play with ideas. It was wonderful to see the way his mind worked. He would get so excited by the ideas he was playing with. He must have been a delight for his students. One of the phrases my friend used was, "What *bugs* me is." He had a bug in his mind much as one might have a cold, infection, or a virus. Why would anything *bug* us? The miracle-minded literally cannot be *bugged*.

*Watch your mind for the scraps of fear,*
*or you will be unable to ask me to do so.*

T-4.III.7:5

### 10. Watch for "Hate," "Fear," "Afraid," and "Fight"

Do we really "hate" some of the things we say we "hate"? Notice the use of the phrase, "I hate it when that happens" or, "I hate to have to say this but . . . " One of my daughter's friends was talking about the way she hated her hair and how she hated the way she was dressed. Another friend said she hated New York City. Are we really afraid it might rain this afternoon? Are there really things in this world we must fight against? Remember, the ways of war are not the ways of peace. Are "hate," "fear," "afraid," and "fight" really the words we want to use?

## Words to Cut Back but Not Completely Eliminate

Most of the above words we can completely eliminate from our vocabulary, just as we might completely cut candy, cookies, cake, and ice cream from our diet. The next group of words we'll probably have to use from time to time, though we can cut back on the frequency and be more conscious of the *context* in which they are used. The thing to notice is whether or not the words are used in a ego-laden and judgmental way. They may be words we need to use, but we don't have to use them so much. We're not completely cutting out these words. Here, we're just going on a more restricted diet not a complete fast.

1. **Watch for "Them" and "They"**
   One morning, I drove a friend to the airport. He wanted to listen to a radio station which gave regular reports on traffic conditions. There was a political commentator making observations about the state of our world along with the constant repetition of the words, "they, they, they, they," "them, them, them, them," Who are "they"? The truth is, there is no "they."

2. **Watch for "Want," "Need," and "Have to Have"**
   Do we really "need" or "have to have" some of the things we may think we "need"? How much of life is governed by the tyranny of needs? While there are times when we may need to go to the grocery store or we may "need" to stop for gas, when I'm in my right mind, do I need for things to be different than they are? Byron Katie (1942–present) has a book called, *I Need Your Love. Is That True?* Wherever

there is a need of this sort there is an ego. Love does not
need anything. Need is an expression of the thought
that something is missing. If I have no needs, I make no
demands upon the world. At one with God, there is never a
moment when we truly lack anything. The miracle-minded
grow progressively away from needing, wanting, or having
to have anything.

Sudden awakenings are rare but possible. One such
description comes from Susan Segal (1945–1997, U.S.),
author of *Collision With the Infinite.* A twenty-seven-year-
old pregnant American woman married to a French doctor,
she was about to board a bus in Paris when . . .

I lifted my right foot to step into the bus and collided head-on with
an invisible force that entered my awareness like a silently explod-
ing stick of dynamite, blowing the door of my usual consciousness
open and off its hinges. What I had previously called "me" was force-
fully pushed out of its usual location inside me into a new location
that was approximately a foot behind and to the left of my head. "I"
was now behind my body looking out at the world without using the
body's eyes.

A seasoned meditator, Susan could not figure out what
had happened. She no longer had any wants or needs, cravings or desires. She found herself being an observer rather
than a projector. She continued to live a normal life but
everything had changed. She started going to psychologists
to find out what had happened, but no one could figure
it out. She was eventually diagnosed with a "dissociative
personality disorder." Not having "wants" or "needs" meant
she no longer had a personality. Finally, one of her ther-
apists decided that she had experienced the disintegration

of the ego, which some might equate with insanity. To a Teacher of God, however, such an egoless state means that one has gained sanity rather than lost it.

3. **Watch for "But"**

> *"You said 'but.' I've put my finger on the whole trouble.*
> *You're a 'but' man. Don't say, 'but.' That little word*
> *'but' is the difference between success and failure."*

SGT. ERNIE BILKO IN *THE PHIL SILVERS SHOW* (FROM THE 1950S)

"But" becomes negative when we use it to reverse whatever we say. When we make a positive statement then follow it with the word "but," we undo what we said in the first phrase. "I love you, but . . ." "You are a good kid, but . . ." This will probably not be perceived as a compliment. We can always tell when a "but" is coming up before it is said. If I say, "It's probably none of my business but." It "probably" is none of my business. Instead of the word "but," put in a period and start a new sentence. Or, substitute the word "and." As a magazine editor, I sometimes have to tell folks that I liked what they wrote and I feel it needs more work. Sometimes we will "need" to say "but." According to the study by Jan Donges, mentioned at the beginning of this chapter, "but" can also be used when we are "trying to be honest," that is, when we are trying not to overlook the details of a description; or, we are trying to look at both sides of a situation. What we're watching out for is the use of but in a critical statement.

4.  **Watch Phrases Suggesting Over-Extension**

    Many of these words relate directly to diet. For example, "I'm stuffed, or "I'm too full," "I overdid it," or, "I can't help myself" are all demonstrations of the lack of our own control and again represent our being out of balance. Sometimes when folks do something inhumane, they excuse themselves by saying they are only human.

5.  **Watch Phrases Suggestive of Bodily or Psychological Response**

    "He makes me sick." "I can't stand it." "He is a pain in the butt." "It drives me crazy." Really, are you being driven crazy? Is that where you want to go?

6.  **Watch for Weasel Words**

    > *I have made every effort to use words that are almost impossible to distort, but it is always possible to twist symbols around if you wish.*

    T-3.I.3:11

    Weasel words are "twists" on words and/or words with double meanings. Weasel words are used to avoid a straight-forward answer. They conceal the truth and are used to manipulate. We say the company is "restructuring" rather than saying people are being fired. The Pentagon speaks about "collateral damage" and "friendly fire" rather than killing people. Soldiers are taught to speak of those they are killing not as people; rather, they are to be called "the enemy." Weasel words include generalizations like, "Many people say . . ." and "The alleged thief . . ." Even the use of the word "alleged" implies that one is a thief.

You can't push someone's buttons if they don't have any buttons to be pushed. Not only are we not to judge, we don't have to be upset if others judge us. This is a real sign of spiritual maturity. Jesus, going to the cross because of others' judgments of him, is an extreme example. He was willing to be crucified to show us that the projections being made upon him didn't matter. Sometimes, we're tested big time. Expect nothing of others and if love comes back our way, we can enjoy it. Keep giving love away, even if it goes unacknowledged.

## Mo Chao—Devise No Words

Bodhidharma (fifth century BCE, China), the founder of Zen Buddhism, says, "Devise no words." In China, they call this state of mind *mo chao*—when we are not projecting. *Mo* means "serene or silent" and *chao* means "awareness." It is a mirror-like quality that just reflects, just sees, just receives—just loves. Jesus, in the gospels says, we should let all of our answers be "Yes," or "No"—all else comes from evil. Watch carefully and see what is being said. In so far as we "live" within the ego-mind, we remain not entirely conscious of why we do what we do. It is possible to awaken from this darkness. A good place to start is to watch the words that come out of our mouths.

> *Be careful of your thoughts,*
> *for your thoughts inspire your words.*
> *Be careful of your words,*
> *for your words precede your actions.*
> *Be careful of your actions,*
> *for your actions become your habits.*
> *Be careful of your habits,*
> *for your habits build your character.*

*Be careful of your character,*
*for your character decides your destiny.*

CHINESE PROVERB

*Your words should reflect only mercy,*
*because that is what you have received*
*and that is what you should give.*

T-3.VI.6:2

# CHAPTER 20

# There Is Nothing to Forgive

## Or, There Is No Future in the Past

*And when the memory of God has come to you*
*in the holy place of forgiveness you will remember nothing else . . .*

T-18.IX.14:1

A Sunday School Teacher asked her class what we must do before we can be forgiven of our sin, expecting someone to say that we must repent of our sins. One young man reached back even further and said, "First you must sin." Someone once said, "No one forgets where the hatchet is buried." We sometimes hear people say, "I can forgive but I cannot forget." We can each probably think of times when something we thought was long forgotten and well buried is very much the topic of conversation, "Remember in 2008, how you lost our money in that horrible investment." It has not been forgotten, so it has not been forgiven. "I can forgive but I cannot forget," is another way of saying, "I will not forgive."

*The ego's plan is to have you see error clearly first,*
*then overlook it, yet how can you overlook what you have made real?*
*By seeing it clearly,*
*you have made it real and cannot overlook it.*

T-9.IV.4:4–6

The ego experiences sin by placing itself in a "holier-than-thou" position from which others may be forgiven for the wrong we think they have done *sometimes*. Witnessing sin is providing testimony to its reality. We cannot forgive a sin we believe is real. Forgiveness requires a complete reversal in thinking. We need a perspective outside the realm of the ego. The ego version of forgiveness is, thus, not forgiveness but judgment masquerading as forgiveness. We cannot then overlook what we make real. In fact, the more clearly we see error, the more we make it real, and the less we are able to overlook it.

The following is a dialogue between a husband and a wife:

> Husband: Why do you keep bringing up my past mistakes? I thought you had forgiven and forgotten.
>
> Wife: I have, indeed, forgiven and forgotten, but I don't want you to forget that I forgave and forgot.

We may offer pardon sometimes but we retain the awareness that the offender has sinned. This process keeps sin alive. The Course asks us to go beyond the appearance. This is admittedly not easy to do and a great struggle while we remain trapped in the ego perspective. Convinced of the reality of "sin" in our brother, it is impossible to see the face of Christ within.

Just before Leonardo da Vinci commenced work on his *Last Supper*, he had a quarrel with a fellow painter. Leonardo was so enraged and bitter that he was determined to paint the face of his enemy, the other artist, into the face of Judas. Thus, would he take his revenge and "vent his spleen," handing the man down in infamy and scorn to succeeding generations. The face of Judas was the first that he finished, and everyone could see it was the face of the painter with whom he had quarreled. When Leonardo came to paint the face of Jesus, he couldn't do it. Something was thwarting his best efforts. Eventually, he painted out the face of Judas and commenced anew on the face of Jesus, this time with success.

We cannot paint the features of Christ into our own life and at the same time paint a brother's face with the colors of enmity and hatred. If we cannot forgive, we cannot see peace. The statement, "May God forgive you your sins" is a strange parody. A loving Father cannot bring condemnation upon us. God cannot forgive sin because God does not condemn (W-46.1:1). In order to have forgiveness, we must first have condemnation. Condemn and we are made prisoners. Forgive and we are set free. There is no forgiveness in Heaven because it's not needed.

There is a story about a Catholic priest who lived in the Philippines, a much-loved man who carried a burden of guilt about a long past sin. He had committed this so-called sin many years before, during his time in seminary. No one knew of it. There was a woman in his parish who claimed she regularly spoke with the Holy Spirit. The priest was skeptical about her claim, so he said, "The next time you talk to the Holy Spirit, ask him what sin it was your priest committed while he was in seminary." The woman agreed and went home. When she returned to church a few days later, the priest said, "Did you ask the Holy Spirit what sin your priest committed in seminary?" "Yes," the woman said, "I asked Him." "Well," said the priest, "What did he say?" The woman responded: "He said, 'I don't remember.'" That is the right answer because the Holy Spirit does not make sin real or seek to compound error. God does not engage in reprisal. God does not know about illusion. We may understand this best in the love we have for our children, when we forgive regardless of what happens.

My friend Rabbi Joseph Gelberman escaped Hitler's growing terror and fled to the United States in 1939, with plans of later bringing along his wife, daughter, mother, father, brothers, and sisters. Two of his brothers also made it to the United States. Everyone else died in the concentration camps, including his wife and daughter. Joseph said his hatred for Hitler was so great, that he finally realized that unless he could rise above it, see the whole thing as the insanity that it was and then forgive it, Hitler was going to wind up killing him too. It took many years for him to do so and it tried his faith, until one day he realized that in order for peace to return to his own mind, he was going to have to let it go. As I write this, he is now ninety-eight years old. Sometimes when I'm asked, "How can I possibly forgive . . . ?" I respond, "You don't have any choice, someday you're going to let it go, so you might as well let it go now." As the Course expresses it, "Why wait for Heaven?" (W-131.6:1)

## Forgiveness Is a Reciprocal Process

As we extend forgiveness, so are we forgiven. The Lord's Prayer says, "Forgive us our debts," then there is the very important word, 'as' "we forgive our debtors." *As* giving is a preface to receiving, and judging is a preface to being judged, *so* forgiveness prefaces our experience of being forgiven. There is nothing to forgive, unless we believe there is. As we forgive by not condemning, we are freed of suffering. In this process, we are healed. As we give, we receive; as we forgive (by not making the error real), so are we forgiven; as we forgive, so do we remember our Oneness and our Home.

There are many incredible examples of forgiveness occurring under the most remarkable of circumstances. During the Korean War, a South Korean civilian was arrested by the communists and ordered shot. But when the young communist leader learned that the prisoner was in charge of an orphanage, he decided to spare him and to kill the South Korean civilian's son instead. So they shot the nineteen-year-old boy in the presence of the father. Later, the fortunes of war changed, and the young communist leader was captured by the United Nations' forces, tried, and condemned to death. But before the sentence could be carried out, the South Korean, whose son had been killed, pleaded for the life of the communist, saying, "He was young. He did not know what he was doing." The United Nations' forces granted his request; and, the South Korean civilian took his son's murderer into his own home.

While God sees no differences among illusions, we certainly do, and forgiving the murder of one's child is about as tough as it gets. There remains, however, no order of difficulty in miracles. One is not bigger or harder than another. If a small thing takes my peace of mind away or a big thing takes my peace of mind away—either way I've lost my peace. Without the love of God in our hearts, it is impossible to forgive. The South Korean man realized that the murderer was acting insanely and did not know what he was doing. If someone is insane, they need our help, not our attack.

## There Is No Future in the Past

To make sin real and then try to forgive it, affirms its reality. Our pardon is then a useless attempt to overlook what we think is true. If we make an illusion real, the pardon we offer the world is a deception. We don't really forgive, and we show that we do not, by hanging on to hurt feelings. The major problem we have in relationship to forgiveness is that we believe we must forgive the truth and not an illusion. If we think that an offense is real, we must then also believe that forgiveness is a lie (W-134.3:1 & 4:2). We demonstrate our knowledge of Heaven by showing others that his or her so-called "sin" does not affect us.

Not being affected by sin, we remove its cause. The Course asks us to teach no one that they can hurt us (T-4.III.8:2). Another way to say this is that time cannot intrude upon eternity—the unreal cannot affect the real. The ego lives in time, constantly rehearsing the past and projecting the future. If there is no past, there is nothing to hang onto. There is nothing to project onto; there is just this moment and there is nothing to forgive in the moment. Forgiveness does not keep time. It ends it.

When missionaries first went to Labrador, they found that the Eskimos had no word for forgiveness. So they made up a word, which in Eskimo was: *Is-suma-gi-jou-jung-naimer-mik* which meant, "Not-being-able-to-think-about-it-any-more." A missionary who asked a young Eskimo girl if she had made her peace with God replied, "I did not know there was any quarrel." In a similar way, Henry David Thoreau on his deathbed was asked by one of his aunts if he had made his peace with God and he said, "We never argued." As the famous English Baptist minister Charles Spurgeon (1834–1882) said it, "When you bury a mad dog, don't leave his tail above ground." The past is the past. To forgive means to let it all go. As we forgive by not condemning, we are freed of suffering. In the realm of the ego, no one forgets where the hatchet is buried. We may pretend that we have forgiven, but we cannot forgive a sin we believe is real.

> *Unjustified forgiveness is attack.*
> *And this is all the world can ever give.*
> *It pardons 'sinners' sometimes,*
> *but remains aware that they have sinned.*
> *And so they do not merit the forgiveness that it gives.*
> *This is the false forgiveness*
> *which the world employs to keep the sense of sin alive.*

T-30.VI.3:5–8 & 4:1

## Forgiveness to Destroy and Forgiveness for Salvation

In *The Song of Prayer*, the pamphlet that came after and from the same source as the Course, a distinction is drawn between forgiveness to destroy and forgiveness for salvation. Forgiveness to destroy is a weapon in the world of form whose purpose is to make what God created equal, different. It has many forms including:

1. **In gracious lordliness a better person stoops to save a lesser one.** This is not true empathy but a form of

arrogance and furthering of separation. We cannot forgive and despise. There is no joining in judgment.

2. **A second form says that both I and my neighbor are deserving of God's wrath.** The martyr makes a show of their humbleness and demonstrates how good they are despite the others cruelty.

3. **Forgiveness to destroy may also take the form of bargaining and compromise.** A cartoon from The New Yorker Magazine shows a woman talking to a friend while her husband sits in a chair in the background and the woman says, "Forgive him? For free?"

Forgiveness for Salvation has one form only. It does not ask for proof of innocence or recompense of any kind. It does not dispute. It does not evaluate the errors to be forgiven. To witness sin and then try to forgive it is backward thinking. Concentration on error is only further error. We demonstrate peace of mind by showing others that their transgressions against us do not have an effect. If there is no effect, there is no cause; nothing happened. We simply thereby demonstrate, as Jesus did, that we cannot be betrayed. It is not difficult to overlook mistakes if we do not give them any effect over us (T-30.VI.10:2). By not being affected by sin, we remove its cause. Jesus did not condemn those who crucified him. Our task is no different than his.

*The major difficulty that you find in genuine forgiveness*
*on your part is that you still believe you must forgive the truth*
*and not illusions. . . For it is impossible to think of sin as true*
*and not believe forgiveness is a lie.*

W-134.3:1 & 4:2

The task is to let go so completely that there is no memory of wrong-doing, because there is nothing in us to make things wrong. If we think that someone has mistreated us, rather than jumping to a defense, can we not realize how he or she has acted out of fear and ignorance? Can we not see mistakes as a call for help?

> . . . you are merely asked to see forgiveness
> as the natural reaction to
> distress that rests on error,
> and thus calls for help.
> Forgiveness is the only sane response.

T-30.VI.2:7–8

Everyone we offer healing to returns it. Everyone we attack holds it against us. The cost of giving is always receiving. God is the only cause and God does not cause guilt. What is not of God has no power over us (T-14.III.8:1f). We would never attack another person, unless we believed they were capable of taking the peace of God from us. No one can take the peace of God from us, unless we give them that power.

> When you forgive the world your guilt, you will be free of it.

T-27.VIII.13:2

## Forgiveness Must Be Total

> Then Peter went up to him and said "Lord, how often must I forgive
> my brother if he wrongs me? As often as seven times?"
>
> Jesus answered, "Not seven, I tell you, but seventy times seven."

MATTHEW 8:21–22

We cannot forgive some people and not forgive others. There cannot be some things we forgive in someone but other things about that same person we cannot forgive. Forgiveness is not something we do sometimes. To forgive "seventy times seven" means to forgive repeatedly—infinitely, no matter how wrong we might think another has been, no matter how many times we may think we have been abused. The answer remains: "Forgive, Forgive, Forgive." "Let it go, Let it go, Let it go."

*You who want peace can find it only by complete forgiveness.*

T-1.VI.1:1

Inner Peace is obtainable when we hold to these ideas:

1. Peace of mind, salvation, and the abundance that comes with it can be our only goal.
2. Through forgiveness, we begin to see everyone, including ourselves, as guiltless. If Jesus, on the cross, can forgive murderers, can we not be more tolerant of lesser sins that we think have been committed against us?
3. As we give up our grievances, we find ourselves becoming increasingly aware of the ever-present, subtle, and gentle guidance of Holy Spirit. Following Holy Spirit, we choose peace of mind over condemnation. As long as we are unforgiving, we can justify the belief that whatever is wrong in the world is caused by something outside of us.

- Justifying even one grievance blocks our own way to the Kingdom.
- As long as we project guilt and sin upon the world, we live in confusion and despair.
- As long as we live in fear, love has no place in our hearts.

## A Practical Test for Forgiveness

If I truly let go and forgive, I come to a realization, "I am the one who is forgiven. I am the one who is liberated. I am the one who is set free. It never had anything to do with the other. What I am letting go of is my own condemnation." This does not mean that the other may not have done something in the world. The world is full of examples of one brother hurting another. It is also full of miracles. Indeed, most miracles remain unseen. How many innumerable acts of forgiveness have occurred about which no one knows anything? As we forgive, we come to know ourselves the way God created us. As we forgive, we experience the Kingdom of Heaven within.

I taught college and university classes for forty years and in that time, I only gave one A+. The woman who earned it was a student in Bedford Prison. Lisa was an absolute delight. She sat in the front row. She was funny and bright. We would often do little forms of "intellectual sparking" with each other. She earned the A+ because she was the only student I ever had who not only read the text book—she also read every book she could get from the New York State library system listed in the bibliography at the end of the text.

As teachers in the prison, we were told not to inquire about our students crimes. If a student voluntarily told you their crime, that was one thing, but we were not to ask. One evening, I was leaving the prison with another teacher and I asked her if she had Lisa as a student and then said, "Isn't she the most wonderful student? She is an absolute joy." And then the other teacher, said, "Yes, you know her crime, don't you? She drowned her daughter in the bathtub." I did not know. What if I had known her crime before the class began? Would I have come to appreciate, even admire her as I did? While working in prison, I got to know many wonderful students as human beings. They made what we would think of as some big mistakes, otherwise, they could not have been there;

but, I got to know them as people not as criminals. Regardless of the egregious nature of our crimes, we are all just people here.

## All Forgiveness Is Self Forgiveness

*As sin is an idea you taught yourself,*
*forgiveness must be learned by you*
*as well, but from a Teacher other than yourself,*
*who represents the other Self in you.*
*Through Him you learn how to forgive the self you think you made,*
*and let it disappear. Thus you return your mind as one to Him*
*Who is your Self, and Who can never sin.*

W-121.6:3–5

It's not up to God to forgive us because God never condemn us. It's up to ourselves to forgive us, which is a very God-like thing to do. In fact, it's the way we come to know God. There really is no one to forgive but ourselves and what we forgive ourselves for is our own misperceptions. We can use a capital "S" when talking about Self-forgiveness, as we are only capable of forgiving ourselves from a higher point of view. The ego cannot forgive. Along with forgiveness comes self-realization. As we forgive so are we forgiven. In the deepest sense, to forgive means to forget—to forget where the hatchet is buried, to let it go to another time, and go on.

*See no one, then, as guilty,*
*and you will affirm the truth of guiltlessness unto yourself.*
*In every condemnation that you offer the Son of God*
*lies the conviction of your own guilt.*

T-13.IX.6:1

## Steps in Forgiveness

1.  **Identify the problem.** I take a good look at what I think my brother has done. I do not deny, repress it, or project it. No one can make me feel, believe, or act in any way. No one can make me angry unless I give them that power. If angered ask, "Why?" What is it I don't want to look at? No one wants to look at their own guilt; and yet, it is not until I look at it that I can release it. Guilt is the thought that I have done something "against God." I tried to create my own world.

2.  **Be Responsible! Let it Go!** It's that simple. It does not matter how big it is or how much our feelings are hurt. We've made "something" out of "nothing." Not until we see this can we "really" let it go. Why hold on to something which hurts? Give the unforgiveness to the Holy Spirit for correction. "Holy Spirit, I have done this thing (getting angry) to myself and it is this I would undo" (T-27.VIII.11:6).

3.  **Stop! Look! Listen!** The Holy Spirit is available right now. Not for a second do I need to wait. Why put it off? We are already saved. God wins in the end so let him win, now. Now really is the only time there is.

4.  **Thank the Holy Spirit** for His help in forgiveness. In so doing, love is shared.

## Forgiveness Is an Illusion

Forgiveness is an illusion because there is nothing to forgive.

> *Illusions makes illusion. Except one.*
> *Forgiveness is illusion that is answer to the rest.*

W-198.2:8–10

Just as Atonement is the only defense that does not lead to further defensiveness, so forgiveness is an illusion that does not lead to further illusion. *Forgiveness is an illusion because there is nothing to forgive.* There is nothing to forgive unless I dream it so. Forgiveness is the end of dreaming. It's awakening. Forgiveness is not the truth, but it points to the truth. Ultimately, we see that forgiveness wasn't necessary. Forgiving the world for what we thought it was, we find our way home again. Salvation is a happy dream in which we forgive all things that no one ever did and overlook what is not there (T-30.IV.7:1–5). Once we have forgiven, we see that forgiveness wasn't necessary; we just thought it was. With the development of miracle-mindedness, we gradually begin to see all of life in a whole different way; and, what once seemed impossible becomes the only way to live.

*Forgiveness, on the other hand, is still, and quietly does nothing.*
*It offends no aspect of reality, nor seeks to twist it to appearances*
*it likes. It merely looks, and waits, and judges not.*

W-PT II.1.4:1–3

Peace of mind occurs as we drop our concern with getting. Drop the need to be right, and concentrate on giving. Only then do we truly receive. Forgiveness is the vehicle for changing our perception and letting go of our fear, condemnations, judgments, and grievances. To think there is something to forgive means making the error real. We teach our brothers and sisters that they cannot hurt us by not making error real.

*The world began when we chose guilt.*
*The world will end when we choose forgiveness.*

DR. KENNETH WAPNICK (1942–PRESENT)

*There is nothing to hold on to.*
*Nothing!*

# CHAPTER 21

# The Key Marked Kindness

## As We Teach, So Do We Learn

*Therefore, God's teachers are wholly gentle.*
*They need the strength of gentleness,*
*for it is in this that the function of salvation becomes easy.*

M-4.IV.2:1–2

*The might of God's teachers lies in their gentleness,*
*for they have understood their evil thoughts*
*came neither from God's Son nor his Creator.*

M-4.IV.2:8

Removing the blocks to the awareness of love's presence, love now unblocked can move freely forth. It is easy to love when none of our own stuff is in the way. Advancing in the Course, we progressively look upon the world from the point of a quiet center.

*This quiet center, in which you do nothing,*
*will remain with you, giving you rest in the midst of every busy*

*doing on which you are sent. For from this center will you be*
*directed how to use the body sinlessly.*

T-18.VII.7:3–5

God has given us a place in His Mind that is forever ours. As arrogance falls away, as guilt and the need for specialness dissipates, as the truth of Being comes more immediately to the fore, so does patience and gentleness grow within.

What is the first quality we think of when we think of Mother Teresa, Gandhi; Martin Luther King Jr., or the Dali Lama? Is it not their kindness? Jesus says in the Gospels that he is "gentle and humble in heart and for this reason his yoke is easy and his burden light" (Matthew 11:29–30). Jesus was kind to the poor, the sick, to children, to prostitutes, to tax collectors, to his accusers, and those who tried and crucified him. He was kind to the soldiers who stood at the foot of his cross and jeered at him and to the thief who died next to him on the cross.

St. Francis of Assisi regarded everything as his brother and his sister, thus, the title of the movie about his life, *Brother Sun, Sister Moon.* He was not interested in owning anything but loved everything and was therefore incredibly rich. All animals, trees, and flowers were friends to St. Francis. His kindness extended so deeply that once when "reportedly" his robe caught fire, and one of his brothers ran to put it out, he said, "No don't hurt brother fire."

*When kindness has left people even for a few moments,*
*we become afraid of them, as if their reason had left them.*

AMERICAN AUTHOR, WILLA CATHER (1873–1947), IN *MY MORTAL ENEMY*

If we are angry, we are insane—our *reason has indeed* left us. Whenever we are angry, upset, disturbed, perturbed, envious, jealous, or projecting in any way, we are not functioning from our right mind and another way of looking at the world is called for. Whenever we're unkind, we see ourselves as separate. When we are kind, we see ourselves as one.

*Kindness is impossible, if you believe in separation.*

DR. KENNETH WAPNICK (1942–PRESENT)

When I perform funerals and interview relatives before the service to gather information for a eulogy, I notice that the first, most positive and powerful thing anyone can say about another human being after they are dead is not that they made a lot of money, built a lot of buildings, or wrote a bunch of books; the main thing is that they were kind: to children, to animals, to everyone. Acts of kindness, gentleness, and benevolence are the best parts of anyone's life. What would you like said for your eulogy? Can you think of anything better than "He or she was kind or gentle?" The best moments in life are those in which we are kind to someone else, or someone is kind to us. Kindness is so big, so beyond us, so powerful, that it is *greater than all wisdom of the wise.* It is, in fact, wiser to be kind than it is to be wise.

*The inclination to goodness is imprinted deeply*
*in the nature of man;*
*insomuch that if it issues not toward men*
*it will take on to other living creatures.*

ENGLISH PHILOSOPHER FRANCIS BACON (1561–1626)

When training an animal, the best way to get an animal to do things is with kindness. They then trust us and willingly share their lives with us. There is nothing softer or thinner than water. But to compel the hard and unyielding, water has no equal. Water gently wears away rocks. In this way, the weak overcomes the strong and the hard gives way to the gentle.

No matter how dark another's heart may *seem*, someplace inside there is a *Real Self*, a gentle, kind being seeking to be free.

*When a brother behaves insanely, you can heal him only by perceiving the sanity in him. If you perceive his errors and accept them, you are accepting yours. If you want to give yours over to the Holy Spirit, you must do this with his.*

T-9.III.5:1–3

Miracle-mindedness knows nothing of fault and error. It is not seen. It is not amplified. It is not lifted out, examined and placed on display for the world to see. To perceive error and then to react to it is to make it real to ourselves. If in doubt about the correct response in any situation, try kindness. It will never fail. Kindness is always appropriate and the moment is always now. To make guilty is to be guilty. Likewise, we cannot do good to another and not benefit ourselves. What we want for a brother—we receive.

*To accuse is not to understand.*

T-14.V.3:6

There is a wonderful story about a prison where they allowed men on death row to have pets. A man with a reputation for hardness and cruelty was given a kitten. He loved and cared for the kitten with tremendous kindness and all because he said, "It was the only thing that ever loved me." The inclination to kindness is easy to give to our pets because they so easily show kindness to us. There is a joke which asks, "If you want to find out who your best friend is, lock your wife and your dog in the trunk of your car. Go away for an hour, come back, open the truck and see which one is happy to see you." As someone once observed, "There is no psychiatrist in the world as good as a puppy licking your face."

When someone is sick, we treat them with kindness. When people are old and crippled, we treat them with kindness. If kindness is the best way to deal with animals, the dumb, the deaf, the lame, the blind, the old, and the sick—why should we think that anger and attack are ever appropriate with our family, friends, and colleagues? God, in the Course, is spoken of as "the maker of the world of gentleness" (T-25.III.8:1). Just as the sun makes ice melt, kindness causes misunderstanding, mistrust, and hostility to evaporate.

Kindness breeds kindness. Kindness blesses the giver and the receiver. Those who bring sunshine into the lives of others cannot keep it from themselves. We are made kind by being kind. When we are kind, we get a magnificent sensation inside. Something inside says, "This is how I should feel all the time." Just as there is no order of difficulty in miracles, there is no such thing as a small act of kindness. Every kindness creates a ripple without end. As we condemn others, so do we condemn ourselves; as we judge others, we judge ourselves. One of the most beautiful compensations of life is that we cannot earnestly help someone else without helping ourselves.

## Forgiveness's Kindness

There is a section in *The Song of Prayer* entitled "Forgiveness of Yourself," which talks about true *forgiveness' kindness* (S-2.I.1:4). We beat up on ourselves more than anyone else does; and, we've not been completely forgiving unless we can, in all kindness, also forgive ourselves. It is a kindness to ourselves to hear God's word and learn His simple lessons instead of trying to dismiss His words, and substitute our own in place of His (W-198.5:3). Being kind to ourselves, we abandon the tyrannical laws of the ego and allow the Holy Spirit to guide our lives. Kindness is such a simple thing. It is not hard to practice. Just as we would be kind with animals, or with the crippled, we can be kind to the customer who just took advantage of our generosity, the discourteous gas station attendant, the thoughtless taxicab driver, the harried waitress. Abraham Joshua Herschel (1907–1972), a Warsaw born American Rabbi and one of the leading Jewish theologians of the twentieth century said, "When I was young, I used to admire intelligent people; as I grow older, I admire kind people."

*Kindness is a language which the dumb can speak*
*and the deaf can hear and understand.*

CHRISTIAN NESTLE BOVE

## Are You Jesus?

A group of salesmen who went to a regional sales meeting in Chicago, assured their wives that they would be home in time for dinner on Friday evening. One thing lead to another and the meeting ran over. The men had to race to the airport. As they barged through the terminal, they inadvertently kicked over a table supporting apples being sold by a young girl. Without stopping, they all reached the plane in time and boarded it with a sigh of relief—all but one. He paused, waved goodbye to his companion and returned to help the girl. He then noticed that she was blind. The salesman gathered up the apples and noticed that several were bruised. He reached into his wallet and said to the girl. "Here, please take this money for the damage we did. I hope we didn't spoil your day." As the salesman started to walk away, the bewildered girl called out to him— "Are you Jesus?"

*The memory of God comes to the quiet mind.*
*It cannot come where there is conflict,*
*for a mind at war against itself remembers not eternal gentleness.*

T-23.I.1:1

No matter how confused we are—no matter how upset or how much we may think the world has mistreated us—there is always an exit. There is a simple law of kindness. It may go by the name of courtesy, charity, mercy, grace, hospitality, or accommodation. The key marked "kindness" can open any door. Love is home. Home is the where the heart is. Eventually, the path of destiny leads us Home. We may get confused in this journey—there are many things to pull us off track—but getting back on track is simple. It just requires the application of one simple law of happiness; the law that says, kindness always works.

*Spread love everywhere you go.*
*Let no one ever come to you without leaving better and happier.*
*Be the living expression of God's kindness:*
*kindness in your face, kindness in your eyes,*
*kindness in your smile, kindness in your warm greeting.*

ALBANIAN CATHOLIC NUN MOTHER TERESA (1910–1997)


*Holiness created me holy.*
*Helpfulness created me helpful.*
*Perfection created me perfect.*
*Kindness created me kind.*

W-PI.67.2:3–6

# Postscript

## Living *A Course in Miracles*

L iving the Course means coming to a quiet place inside; it means obtaining objectivity. Forgiving ourselves guilt dissipates and the disruptive past fades from view. Our equilibrium cannot be shaken. Illusions leave us unmoved and undisturbed (T-24.IV.3:3). Someone does something that is blatantly selfish and it does not take our peace away. A waiter is discourteous; someone cuts us off on the road ahead, and peace of mind remains a constant.

Living the Course we learn not to "react" to the world. This does not mean that we do not respond to it. It does mean, however, that I do not give it power over me. Knowing that only "God is" and having placed our faith in God, then even though temptations come our way, though economic challenges, or bodily disorders present themselves, peace of mind remains. Practicing these principles, the eyes become quieter and the forehead more serene; it is easier to have perspective and laughter appears more often. Now I can say, "How silly to think the ego's game was ever real." God's presence is now more consistently and clearly seen. Let God take the reins. Get out of the way and enjoy the ride.

On May 9, 2001, after the doctor said, "Mr. Mundy, I have to tell you that the cancer has spread." I picked up my copy of the Course and read the following lines from Lesson 189. It will always be one of my favorite passages and with it, I close.

*Simply do this: Be still,*
*and lay aside all thoughts of what you are and what God is;*
*all concepts you have learned about the world;*
*all images you hold about yourself.*
*Empty your mind of everything it thinks is either true or false,*

*or good or bad, of every thought it judges worthy,*
*and all the ideas of which it is ashamed. Hold on to nothing.*
*Do not bring with you one thought the past has taught,*
*nor one belief you ever learned before from anything.*
*Forget this world, forget this course,*
*and come with wholly empty hands unto your God.*

W-189.7:1-5

# Resources

If you enjoyed this book, you might enjoy *Miracles* Magazine (Jon Mundy, PhD, publisher, www.miraclesmagazine.org, 845-496-9089). Details of the life of Helen Schucman, Bill Thetford, and the scribing of the Course can be found in Dr. Kenneth Wapnick's *Absence from Felicity*, Dr. Neal Vahle's *A Course in Miracles: The Lives of Helen Schucman and William Thetford*, Robert Skutch's *Journey Without Distance*, D. Patrick Miller's *The Complete Story of the Course*, Carol M. Howe's *Remembering to Laugh: Personal Reflections of Bill Thetford*, and my earlier book, *Missouri Mystic*.

There are a number of different *A Course in Miracles* leaders, organizations, conferences, etc. It is easy to find more information simply by looking online.

**The Foundation for Inner Peace**, www.acim.org
Publishers of *A Course in Miracles*
P.O. Box 598
Mill Valley, CA 94942-0598

**The Foundation for *A Course in Miracles*,** www.facim.org
41397 Buecking Drive
Temecula, CA 92590-5668
951-296-6261

**Miracles Distribution Center**, www.miraclecenter.org
Sells Course-related books and they maintain a list
of Course study groups.
3947 E. La Palma Avenue
Anaheim, CA 92807
714-632-9005

**The Institute for Personal Religion**
Publishers of *Miracles* Magazine, www.miraclesmagazine.org
P.O. Box 1000
Washingtonville, NY 10992
845-496-9089

**Community Miracles Center**, www.miracles-course.org
2269 Market Street
San Francisco, CA 94114

**One Mind Foundation**
ACIM Radio and ACIM Gather, www.acimgather.org
P.O. Box 11
Hastings on Hudson, NY 10706

**Miracles Network**, www.miracles.org.uk
Flat 12a, Barness Court, 6/8 Westboune Terrace,
London, W2 3UW, United Kingdom

**Rocky Mountain Miracles Center**, www.miraclescenter.org
1939 S. Monroe Street
Denver, CO 80210

**Pathways of Light**, www.pathwaysoflight.org
13111 Lax Chapel Road
Kiel, WI 53042,
800-322-7284

**The Circle of Atonement**, www.circleofa.com
P.O. Box 4238
West Sedona, AZ 86340
928-282-0790

**Foundation for the Awakening Mind**, www.awakening-mind.org
4443 Station Avenue, Rear Building
Cincinnati, OH 45232
513-898-1364 (Peace House)

**Course in Miracles Society**, www.jcim.net
7602 Pacific Street, Suite 200
Omaha, NE 68114

**MiraclesOne Foundation**, www.miraclesone.org
Madison, WI

**A Center for Inner Peace**, www.acenterforinnerpeace.com
P.O. Box 150538
San Rafael, CA 94901
415-382-1888

**Love Communications**, www.lovecomm.org
P.O. Box 1023
Belleville, MI 48112

**St. Louis ACIM Leadership Council**, www.acimstlouis.org

**Open Doors**, www.opendoorsclassroom.com

**Be the Love**, www.bethelove.us

# Acknowledgments

D r. Helen Schucman, Dr. William Thetford, and Dr. Kenneth Wapnick introduced me to *A Course in Miracles* in April 1975. Ever since, Ken has been a wise older brother and a gentle guide in my understanding of the Course. I wrote an article about Ken in 1991 titled "Impeccably on the Path." More than twenty years later, he remains as impeccable as ever. We are all indebted to Ken and his wife, Gloria, for the example they set in living *A Course in Miracles.*

My thanks to Judy Whitson, of the Foundation for Inner Peace, for her friendship of over forty years; it was Judy who suggested this project and helped with the connections that made it possible. My assistant Fran Cosentino helped in every stage of development. I am grateful to her for her editorial skills, diligence, and patience. I'm very appreciative for the help of three *Course in Miracles* student/teachers: Ken Mallory, Pauline Edward, and Jean Weston, each of whom read through the entire text and offered their commentaries. Four other good friends and fellow Course student/teachers, Pamela Silberman, Marty Manson, Janet Ladowski, and Lorraine Coburn read through selected chapters.

My friend Shanti Rica Josephs has, since 1972, been my steady rock; the one to whom I've been able to pour out my soul; the one who has consistently known the right answer.

I am grateful for the consistent, kind guidance from my agent, Ivor Whitson, his wife, Ronnie, and my editors at Sterling Publishing, Michael Fragnito and Kate Zimmermann.

Finally, my gratitude to my darling Dolores, for her ever-present love and devotion; the day I met Dolores was the best day of my life.

# About the Author

Jon Mundy, PhD, is an author, lecturer, and, as Dr. Baba Jon Mundane, a standup philosophical comedian. He taught university courses in philosophy and religion from 1967 to 2009. He is the publisher of *Miracles* magazine, the author of nine books, and Senior Minister Emeritus of Interfaith Fellowship in New York City. He met Dr. Helen Schucman, the scribe of *A Course in Miracles*, in 1973. Helen introduced Jon to the Course and served as his counselor and guide until she became ill in 1980.